MOVE!

MOVE!

FROM WHERE YOU ARE TO
WHERE YOU WANT TO BE

Dallas Burnett

Thrive
Publishing, LLC

Thrive Publishing, LLC
PO Box 443
Campobello, SC 29322
www.ThinkMoveThrive.com

Ordering Information:
Quantity sales. Special discounts are available on quantity purchases by corporations, associations, and others. For details, contact the publisher at the address above. Orders by U.S. trade bookstores and wholesalers. IngramSpark Distribution: Tel: US and Canada: +1 (855) 99SPARK or (855) 997-7275 United Kingdom: +44 808 164 8277 Australia: +61 3 9765 4800

Printed in the United States of America

Publisher's Cataloging-in-Publication data
Burnett, Dallas.
MOVE!: From Where You Are to Where You Want to Be / Dallas Burnett.

ISBN-13: 978-1-7325353-0-5
BUS106000 BUSINESS & ECONOMICS / Mentoring & Coaching.
EDU008000 EDUCATION / Decision-Making & Problem Solving

First Edition

001-1118-53-0-5

Dedicated to my best friend,
Danielle

Contents

Preface

The Broken Formula

For two years, I ran a startup company for a private equity firm. The new company had its challenges, but as an entrepreneur, I enjoyed the daily fires and problems that needed immediate attention. It had been a very exhausting and exhilarating two years. We grew fast, and our product was very sought after in the industry. The company was able to hire some amazing people, and we showcased our products with pride.

However, one Monday all of what the team had built changed. Due to circumstances out of our control, I resigned a few days earlier. My expectations about work and business did not match my reality.

Old expectations:
"hard work + great product + a little luck = success"

Reality:
"hard work + great product + a little luck = unemployed"

I was heading to the office to tell the team I would no longer be leading the company. Even worse, I was going to tell the team their jobs were moving to another city and unless they wanted to move, they were being laid off.

What a way to start the week. It was one of the worst days of my life. It was the day I entered into what I refer to as a "Now what?" moment.

My "Now what?" Moment

As I moved through the difficult time of unemployment, this book emerged. It was truly one of the strangest times of my life and career. And it all happened while I was going through a "Now what?" moment.

And just what is a *"Now what?"* moment?

Well, it's that moment that gives you a deep feeling of uncertainty. The chaos of the unknown that seeps into your being. You don't have a plan. You don't have the answers. In fact, you may have already tried your plan or your solutions and failed. You feel as though you may be out of options or not even know what options are available. You feel like areas in your life may be out of control. So you sit down, take a deep breath and say to yourself, "Now what?"

Consider this: I frequently fly for business and love that top-of-the-world view, watching cities and fields and rivers pass below. Sometimes, the plane flew between perfectly white clouds, layered in the sky, and I watched as the familiar things that mark moving forward, or moving period, disappeared. There were no buildings, no fields, no cars. Only white space.

During that time, I could see nothing. No orientation points. No perspective. Only an endless white space. When I transitioned out of the startup I felt directionless for the first time in years.

Movement Through Moments

For as long as I can remember I have set goals, and then moved toward them in a systematic way. Over the years, I learned my strengths and weaknesses. But I found myself in unfamiliar territory, where the life tools I had used and trusted seemed inadequate or lacking. I needed to reorient my life and set a new course during a challenging and confusing season. I needed a system or a process that would help guide me safely through the confusion I faced.

"Now what?" moments show up everywhere: deciding what to do after college graduation; struggling to save your marriage; wondering how to handle a child or teen in trouble; fighting the effects of addiction. "Now what?" moments occur in work and life. Maybe you have a great job, but you are disoriented because it no longer excites you? Is your business struggling? Have you hit a personal plateau?

Instead of starting with solutions like setting goals, working harder, or seeking more advice, I decided to understand the problem. The real problem was not sliding into a little chaos, like my flight slid into some clouds during the flight. My real problem was how to *navigate through* the clouds and *land the plane successfully* without crashing. There was a huge gap between the plane inside the disorienting clouds, and the plane sitting at the terminal gate.

When I discovered how to close gaps that existed in my life, I realized that this is the essence of movement: being able to close the gap between where you are and where you want to be.

The Notebook

Years prior to my leading the startup company, I began a notebook of ideas and concepts that were centered around the idea of movement. My notebook contained years of original thoughts and ideas. On my last day in the office, I stepped out of a hallway and into our resource closet to take a phone call. I laid my notebook on a shelf.

After the call, I found what I needed in the closet and hurried to my next task on that very busy day. I didn't realize I had left behind years of personal reflection and concept notes sitting on a shelf.

Weeks went by and I frantically searched for my favorite notebook that held thoughts that had become almost like treasured thoughts. I continued to search and continued to come up empty-handed until one last visit to the office resulted in my finding it. I felt like Gollum from the Lord of the Rings. My precious!

The turmoil I felt about losing all the wisdom and knowledge I had gained in the notebook propelled me to write this book. I realized that if I was devastated to lose those thoughts about the topic of movement, then I should capture these life-changing, albeit simple, ideas within the following pages.

MOVE! contains wisdom collected over many years of personal experiences and thoughts on how to create movement. I developed the material and system over years of study and coaching employees, and from experiences leading fast-paced startup companies to coaching a first-grade girls' soccer team.

I remember the somewhat cheesy commercial where a guy says, "I'm not just the president of Hair Club for Men, I'm also a client!"

Well, I am not just a writer on movement, I myself needed to move! I am writing this book for everyone facing "Now what?" moments that are suffocating our lives, immobilizing us. The concepts from my notebook and models I discovered helped me land my next venture, and became a central theme in my life, as well as the heart of every coaching session, consulting engagement, parenting strategy, marriage responsibility, and leadership opportunity.

The wisdom contained in the following pages has been instrumental in shaping my personal life. I have shared it with coworkers and friends with whom I have had the privilege to coach or mentor over the years. This wisdom is now summarized in MOVE! – and I truly hope that others find the same help and hope by reading and using it to navigate the white spaces in their lives . . .

Introduction

MOVE! is a book that is concerned with one main idea: Helping you reorient your life systematically to generate meaningful movement towards where you want to be.

If you lie down at the end of the day, feeling discouraged and restless, like it's impossible to accomplish what you hoped–MOVE! was written for you. Going through major life transitions requires you to evaluate numerous opportunities, but the multitude of choices can make it difficult to formulate good decisions. The book will not only help you cut through the mental clutter by asking insightful questions, but also provide applicable wisdom in every chapter.

When you are stuck in a rut, managing change, or facing important life-altering decisions, you need more than a pat on the back. You need a **system** with a **common language** that helps organize your mind on how to view each "Now what?" moment; you need time talk about it with others; and you need confidence as you take each step forward.

A Language of Movement

The system developed in MOVE! is not a quick fix or a plug-n-play. It is a reliable, customizable set of tools that helps you **focus on what is important** as you make your way through difficult problems. It may sound counter-intuitive, but most people have not taken the time to ponder the great question of what they really want in life.

In school we learn a lot of facts. The meaning of adverbs, how to balance equations, and significant battles in history. However, what is lacking in much of our education is instruction on how to *think*. The following pages present a framework that will help you organize your thoughts and align your actions to produce *meaningful* movement, or direction in your life.

There are four main sections of the book that are referred to as "Pillars." The first of the 4 Pillars of Movement is the concept of clarity. What is clarity? What are actionable steps we can take to increase our clarity? How do we gain clarity from a state of confusion? In the following chapters, you will learn seven techniques to generate more clarity while confronting life's many problems.

The last three Pillars of the book leverage the power of clarity to focus our efforts, measure our results, and maintain a winning mindset. We discover how the powerful paradox of *limiting certain activities* can *create greater movement* in our lives. We will learn to answer the question: "How do I know that I know?" and how the answer helps us respond, rather than react, to problems. Finally, the book will walk through the experience of living with a Movement Mindset.

MOVE! seeks to wrap a common language around the process of gaining clarity and focus, making it easier to have a conversation with a friend, mentor, manager, or coach. If you struggle setting boundaries in your life, this book will give you a language to talk through your needs, mentally wrestle with possible solutions, and receive encouragement from others.

Under the Surface

My wife and I were sitting in our car one beautiful day in early May. Normally, we would be excited to have free time to spend together. But not that day.

INTRODUCTION

We were there because we were expecting a phone call that could change our lives. When the phone rang, I answered then heard the nurse ask, "Dallas, are you sitting down?" Before the call, I had spent the morning drinking that awful chalky liquid before having an MRI.

She continued. "Your appendix has ruptured and it's pouring dangerous infection into your body. Listen to me carefully – this is serious. Please get to the hospital now. The surgeon will be waiting for you in the emergency room. You will be immediately taken into surgery."

My wife overheard the nurse and had already started the car and was driving toward the hospital as I hung up the phone.

I couldn't stop thinking about the irony of the situation. I looked perfectly fine on the outside and could function, and yet I was a dead man walking. A lethal concoction was slowly seeping into my system. Without immediate attention, my body would become septic and shut down. It was a sobering thought for a 35-year-old with a wife and three young daughters.

Looking back, I realized that if I had just *faced* the nagging problem, a general feeling of sickness, instead of dismissing or ignoring it, I wouldn't be racing to the hospital.

My problem was not simply my ruptured appendix. **My core problem was that I had consciously ignored the symptoms of my appendicitis** – a problem that was important and required attention. By refusing to address it, I would look like a perfectly healthy 35-year-old man – until the day I dropped dead.

Maybe I was afraid to admit I had a problem. Maybe I was just hoping it would go away on its own. No matter the reason, I was **stuck** with my appendicitis problem until I *decided* to **move**.

C.S. Lewis, one of the greatest theologians and writers of the 20th century, wrote:

"We can ignore even pleasure. But pain insists upon being attended to."[1]

MOVE! will provide you with solid tools to help you identify problems, chart a path forward, and create resolving movement in your life. If you are open and honest with yourself, the questions contained in the book will ensure your problems don't fester beneath the surface and become infected, threatening your life and all you work toward.

What if you discover that one or more of the topics covered reveals a blind spot or weakness in your personality? No worries. Just take time to digest and absorb the weakness and share the idea with a trusted friend, mentor or family member. Please don't ignore it. **Only you can admit "where it hurts." That is your work.**

The material in MOVE! is less instruction and more a reminder of the resources you already have within you. You will find that MOVE! offers simple guidance you can apply to virtually any problem or area in your life. If you are stuck in a rut, facing a difficult decision, or need help understanding how to close the gaps in your life then MOVE! will help.

This is the beginning of the journey that will help you create the rest of your life and even thrive through those pesky "Now what?" moments. For more visual tools to help you remember key messages from each of the Four Pillars of Movement, additional resources, and fun freebies visit: **www.ThinkMoveThrive.com/ resources**.

Chapter 1

The Gap

I respect the man who knows distinctly what he wishes. The greater part of all mischief in the world arises from the fact that men do not sufficiently understand their own aims. They have undertaken to build a tower, and spend no more labor on the foundation than would be necessary to erect a hut.

— John Wolfgang Van Goethe

I was drowning—literally. Sucking in salt water, straining with all my strength, and holding a 9-year-old girl under my left arm. I could see the shore. I knew how far I had to swim to make it. But for the first time in my life, the shield of an invincible 19-year-old was shattered. This thought crossed my mind, "There is a real possibility that my arms and legs are going to give out before we reach the shore, and this girl and I are going to die."

During college, I worked at a camp on the east coast. Twelve college students cut the grass, were lifeguards at the pool, served drinks in the Sea Shack, and played in the ocean as much as possible. It was a great job!

One of the groups staying at the camp had gone out to the beach and were playing games on the beach. A few had braved the water that day, but the undertow was terrible. They had asked me to come along when I got off work.

9

When I got to the beach, one of the leaders asked me if I could help one of the girls who was still in the water. He said, "I don't think she can hear us. Can you wade into the water and tell her it's time to play the game?"

By the time I was waist deep into the surf, I could see that the girl was in trouble. She was barely keeping her head out of the water and was quickly moving further out in the ocean. I felt the tide pulling really hard. Not a rip tide, but still very powerful and dangerous.

Now we were both in trouble. What amazed me was that no one on the shore had a clue about what was going on. They were busy laughing, running, and playing games, while we were fighting to survive less than 100 yards away. I had training on how to deal with rip currents and knew that it was futile to fight against it. But I was also 19, and the shore seemed so close.

Right before I gave out, a series of waves crashed over our heads. We used them to make it to a place where I could get a footing in the sand. It was a miracle, but we both came out sputtering and splashing, thankful to be on dry ground.

When I was in the water I learned a lesson about gaps. A gap is the distance between what *is* and what *could be*. When we move, we exert energy to close the gap. I was drowning; and the difference between life and death was a gap of no more than a few car lengths.

> Gaps create tension. This tension feels like dissonance in our being.

Gaps are problems; like not having enough money to start a business or living through a crummy childhood. We all have problems in life: Limiting problems, scary problems, confusing problems, complicated problems, problems that affect our physical, emotional, professional, relational or financial lives, problems that keep us from becoming or attaining what we really want, problems that keep us from closing the gap between where we are and where we want to be.

We know something isn't right. We look at the world, and we look at our lives, and we think, "I know this can be better." We want the song to end on a pleasing note, but dissonance and tension make the song end before notes resolve. We want to create a product for our business, remodel our master bathroom, or change the way we respond to stressful situations.

We know where we are, but we aren't where we want to be.

My wife was recently talking to a friend who commented on feeling overwhelmed and scattered.

"I am working 50 hours a week, my husband is starting a business, and we have a 3-year-old boy who is having discipline problems at daycare. I get home at night and don't feel like I have any energy left to give to my son and husband. When I am at work, I feel like I should be at home. When I am at home, I feel like I have work I need to get done. I just feel scattered. I know our family is not in a good place, and it's taking its toll on me and my marriage."

My wife's friend was expressing all the problems swirling in her life that were creating chaos. Can you feel the tension she and her husband were feeling? It's no surprise they were both responding with frustration, exasperation, and confusion.

She was able to see all the circumstances floating around in her life, but she could not figure out how to close the gaps to move toward a better life.

~~~~

Several years ago I bought a 1978 Ford pickup truck. I told my wife I needed a truck to drive around our small farm, and that actually was part of the reason I bought it.

When I was a boy, those were the trucks I first remember riding in or by on the highway. To be honest, the other part of the reason I bought that old pickup was the feeling of some inner responsibility to see it brought back to its' original glory.

Why did I care about slowly bringing it back to tip-top shape? Maybe it was a way to see something restored that reminded me of a simpler time. Maybe it was because we both came into being the same year. If it can be restored or renewed, it gives me hope that as my body ages and aches from all those high school sports injuries, I can somehow be restored and renewed over time too.

Just like the pain of my appendicitis and my old Ford pickup, we realize there is a gap that needs traversing.

Just like my old Ford needed restoration and my appendix needed surgery – there is a gap from where we are and where we need or want to be – and we need a force that will help us overcome that gap.

> **Gaps in our lives are the distance between where we are and where we want to be.**

For artists, closing the gap is like the quest to capture beauty and express it in their work flawlessly and uniquely. For the student, it is not only achieving a degree but landing the "perfect job." For the addict, it is achieving freedom from the plague of isolation, confusion, lies, and abuse that is their present reality.

Closing gaps means moving our lives from a place of chaos to more order. Moving our lives from a white space to a colorful canvas. Moving our lives from worn out to renewed. We talk about aspects of movement every day but just use different language.

At work, we use phrases like strategic planning, increasing quality and using Lean Six Sigma, turning around a failing company or setting company goals. We question constantly. How do we create a winning culture? How can we make our product more affordable? How can we make our product more valuable?

At home, we talk about how to get along with our mother-in-law or how our husband is disengaged and needs motivating. We discuss methods of how we can help our kids grow into young men and women of character. We ask our friends to help hold us accountable to work out, stop drinking, or whether we should go out with that guy or girl on a second date.

> *Movement is birthed when you understand where you are and where you want to be. It's knowing you are not there today, and then choosing to close the gap.*

The following paragraphs cover some examples of gaps in our work and lives.

Gaps in Awareness

Great leaders are self-aware. They have an ability to know their strengths and weaknesses. They know their vulnerabilities. They can look at their lives from the outside in. Even if a leader is introspective, he or she will surround themselves with trusted advisors who can help them better understand hidden areas of their life. Their goal is to define the *reality* of every situation, not how they want it to be.

However, it's not just CEOs or Generals who benefit from awareness, we all do.

Judson Brewer, Ph.D. worked for the Department of Psychiatry at Yale's school of medicine, researching how to help people escape addiction. According to Brewer, addiction is caused when we engage in a behavior and associate it with a positive outcome.[2] When our mind experiences the positive outcome, we lay down the neural pathways that give us the desire to experience it again and again.

In Brewer's research, he trained patients on meditation techniques in mindfulness. Mindfulness meditation is an exercise where you learn to train your mind to focus on the present moment. That goal allows you to learn, with practice, how to live beyond past events, like how you were bullied in elementary school, or future worries like making next month's mortgage payment.

What did Brewer's research find? People were twice as likely to quit smoking if they were trained in mindfulness meditation.

How is that possible?

Brewer sums up the answer by quoting one of the participants: "Mindful smoking = smells like stinky cheese and tastes like chemicals. YUCK!"

Instead of feeling like the Marlboro Man and creating that false reality, the participant had been able to see that smoking actually made them smell like "stinky cheese."

When we increase our awareness, it gives us a new perspective on the world around us. We see ourselves as we really are. We see all the good things and all the less than admirable qualities we exhibit. Gaps in our awareness cause us all kinds of problems, but when we can step back and open our eyes, great things happen.

Motivational speaker and coach Tony Robbins echoed the same idea back in 2005 during an interview with Larry King on CNN. While discussing why New Year's resolutions did not work, Robbins said:

> It's more than a wish. It's a hope. It's what I think I should do and it's often a reaction to what we don't like. And when you really resolve something the shift in that is real because here there's an identity shift.
>
> It's kind of like when people say to me, "Well, I've not smoked a cigarette for ten days." and I'll say, "Why are you counting, so you can tell people how many days you lasted when you go back?"
>
> Because when you're a person who's made a shift in your identity, you're not a smoker anymore. It's not a fight anymore

like trying to smoke or not smoke. You just say, "I'm not a smoker."
If somebody offered you a cigarette, you wouldn't say what brand
is it? You'd say, "No, it's not who I am."[3]

Gaps in Knowledge

I appreciate people who have achieved some level of success, and could have a reason to be arrogant and cocky, but instead choose to remain humble and genial.

I was having a conversation with a speaker at a national conference. The topic was very technical. The speaker did an outstanding job communicating the information. You could tell he was off-the-chart intelligent. I complimented his lecture, stated that he was brilliant, and that I could see why he had earned a Ph.D. He made a comment I will never forget: "You know, a Ph.D. is no big deal. I mean, all it says is that I know a lot about a little."

Wow. I sat amazed at his humility shortly after giving and being praised for a technical presentation to a group of industry professionals. It made him relatable to everyone that did not have a Ph.D. and at the same time did not diminish the fact that he knew a lot of information within his chosen field. I respected his attitude about the value of knowledge, but his words and humility showed he valued people too. If a Ph.D. is telling everyone in the room that he has spent his whole life "learning" and still only knows a lot about a little, then we can rest assured that when we face new challenges, we usually have a severe gap in the knowledge required to create movement in our lives.

Gaps in Courage

To complete one of my courses, I landed an interview with a very successful turnaround executive. A turnaround executive is a person that is brought in by a bank or investors when a business begins to fail or files for bankruptcy. When it is time for a cleanup crew, the turnaround professional goes to work.

This executive had turned around several large corporations, taking them from losing money to making money again, in a very short period of time—essentially saving the company and the employees' jobs. I spent 2 hours at lunch with him trying to gain insights into how he approaches problems and how he generated so much movement. Why was *he* able to take the company to profitability so quickly, while the other guy drove it over the fiscal cliff?

He shared one of the major reasons. When he goes into any business that is performing poorly, he looks for the "pet projects." He said it never failed that someone would have an idea and implement it in the company. The idea would not work and would be losing money inside the company. However, for whatever reason, maybe to save face or ignorance or just pride, the CEO would continue to turn a blind eye to the pet project until it ultimately bankrupted the company. This turnaround professional said finding and eliminating the pet project was the number one step he took when planning his turnaround strategy.

We tend to ignore things in our lives that are close to our hearts, our personal "pet projects." We may be blind to them. We may say to ourselves, "It is not that bad, I am sure that other things are causing a majority of the problems. I can create movement in my life if I work on other areas without giving up my pet project." Many times we know exactly what needs to be done, but fear the fallout from our peers.

> *Lacking the courage to address an issue inhibits movement.*

Gaps in Capability

In 2005, I took a call from the Tampa Bay Desalination Water Treatment plant project director, Eric Sabolsice. He was managing construction operations on the largest desalination water plant in the U.S. A desalination plant takes salt water, like ocean water, and converts it into drinking water.

Eric asked for help with a dilemma: "Dallas, I need to dose 100 parts-per-million of calcium hydroxide to complete the water treatment process before it leaves the plant. I have to keep the turbidity (cloudiness) under 1 NTU. Can your system guarantee those results?"

The amount of chemical dosage he was asking for our system to provide was more than *four times* our maximum recommended dosage. We built the most advanced calcium dosing systems in the water treatment industry, but his need far exceeded our capabilities at the time.

I was honest and told him no one in the world could feed those levels of calcium hydroxide and keep the turbidity that low. It was impossible. Yet I also told Eric that I would talk to our team and see if we could help him out in any way.

I thought about Eric's problem, and about our processes and equipment, and how they were not good enough. The light bulb went off for me when I realized that in certain groundwater aquifers, nature produced water that was exactly like the parameters Eric needed. If nature can produce the water, there would be a way that we could too.

At that moment, I no longer accepted the *status quo* that limited me from chasing the solution. I changed my intentions and aimed to solve the problem.

> ✴ **Movement is seeded in the rejection of the status quo.**

We started brainstorming and talking to everyone about possible options. We developed a method in the lab that successfully achieved the desired results. With a lot of help from the team, we assembled a makeshift pilot plant that would run similar to Eric's plant and used the new treatment technology.

It was an absolute disaster. The pilot plant never ran for more than 5 minutes. I tried a dozen variations and got nowhere.

After some time and a few more failures, I thought I had missed something in the lab. I decided to start from scratch to see if I could catch my mistakes.

During one of my experiments, I had a beaker full of water spinning on a stir plate. I had added our chemical and was about to pour it over a filter when I got a phone call. Fortunately for me, the call went long – really long. In fact, I left the beaker on the stir plate spinning for over half an hour.

When I came back, I was frustrated because I was going to have to start all over again but thought I might as well test this water to get a baseline for the next test. When I read the test results on the turbidity meter, I almost fell on the floor.

I had accidentally discovered a technique that would ultimately lead to the solution to Eric's problem.

Seven years of research led to the company filing for the patent and it took another three years before the patent was granted. Seven years of getting it wrong before we got it right. A decade spent closing one gap to help deliver safe drinking water.

> *What in your life is worth the dedication and stamina of working seven years to get it right?*

If we had shut down testing after the first embarrassing display on the pilot unit, we never would have gained all the new knowledge we earned searching for a solution. And I wonder about the phone call that occurred when the beaker was stirring. Could I have solved the problem without that providential break?

That is movement. Intentional and deliberate action in a clear direction. When you change your intentions or aims, you can begin to create movement on a new path.

These are just a few of the many gaps we navigate in our lives.

We have relational gaps with our spouse or family, financial gaps, gaps in our business process or product offering, health gaps, time gaps, age gaps, stage gaps, gap after gap after gap.

MOVE! was created to help you clearly and effectively close the gaps.

Beginning the Journey

The previous chapters have laid the foundation and presented a common language around the concept of movement. We have investigated and answered questions like:

- What is movement?
- What are gaps we face in life?

Now, you need a game plan. A strategy. A game plan is more than just following rules and checking boxes. It is how you apply your strengths and weaknesses creatively within the rules of the game. How do you exploit your opponent's weakness? By using a game plan!

The game plan can be as simple or as complex as needed, depending on the game and situation. The same is true in our lives. We need a game plan, strategy or method on how to approach the problems, transitions, decisions, opposing forces, and gaps in our lives. Using a plan helps guide us through the process. It helps us answer questions like "What do I do now?" or "What comes next?"

Using a game plan or strategy helps us organize our thoughts and align them with our actions. It keeps us focused because we spend less time worrying if we are doing the right thing and more time executing.

Our lives are complicated.

When we face difficult or complicated situations, they can cloud our ability to discern what needs to be done. We may want to "Just Do It," but we don't know exactly what to do. By using a game plan or strategy, it is possible to cut through even the most complicated situations and understand how to proceed.

The mental strategy needed to create movement in your life, business, or relationships is simple.

If you can understand and organize your mind around the framework below, you will create meaningful movement and close many of the gaps that you face in life.

The Four Pillars of Movement are listed in order, as follows:

1. Seek Clarity
2. Develop Boundaries
3. Elevate Accountability
4. Intentionally Execute

This framework simplifies coaching employees, talking to your boss, working through a difficult situation with your kids, deepening your relationship with your spouse, growing your business, or deciding what to eat for lunch.

Once you master these four concepts you will not only be able to close the gaps in your life, you will begin to see how problems relate to the Four Pillars of Movement.

Moving is built on a strong foundation, with each of the following four parts acting as a cornerstone.

Pillar I
Seek Clarity

T. H. BLAIR.
PHOTOGRAPHIC CAMERA.

No. 362,599.   Patented May 10, 1887.

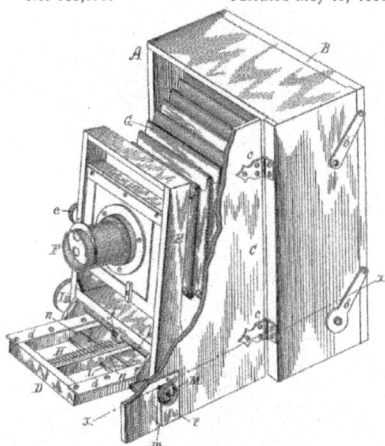

fig. 1

If a man knows not what harbor he seeks, any wind is the right wind.

– Seneca

———————————

I was about to step up to a microphone under bright lights on a smoky stage. Part of me wanted to throw up, another part of me wanted to jump up and down with excitement. I was in uncharted territory. In front of thousands of people, a band was going to play my original song. I was onstage, about to perform the song, without a sound check or practice with the band – and having never performed it in front of anyone. Not once.

No pressure, right?

The audience was full of amazing people. Veterans and their families had come to the first American Freedom Festival in New York City to see a show in their honor. Backstage the acts included Maxim Magazine models, professional WWF wrestlers, country music stars, political commentators, Sean Hannity and Al Franken, American Idol performers – and me.

So, how did I get into this pickle?

For years I had written songs as a hobby. Inspired as a teenager by artists like James Taylor, Bill Withers, and Steve Winwood, I wrote songs as a way to express my thoughts. It was a release and through college helped me deal with stress. When I was 25,

I decided to submit a song to a national contest. This contest, sponsored by Proctor and Gamble, stood out to me because it did not have a cash prize. It was experiential. They would fly the winner to New York, produce the winner's song, and then let the winner play the song on stage with Charlie Daniels. How fun is that! The entry fee was low, so I jumped in. It was the first contest submission I had ever completed.

I decided to write a new song specifically for the contest and not use one that I had written already. They listed the names of the judges (two were recording artists), and I thought I could write a song that sounded like something they would play or sing. It was harder than I thought!

For a month, I would come home at night and hammer away with ideas and melody lines with no success. The night before I had to send in the video I was disappointed. I told my wife I might not send a song into the contest. She said, "You are trying too hard. Write about something you know." I started thinking and decided that I knew about our relationship. I know how we got together. How about our first date?

It was like a lightning bolt hit me. I had perfect clarity. The whole song was written in less than 30 minutes. My wife recorded me on a small video camera, and we sent in the video the next day. Within just a few weeks I went from sitting on my back porch, with my wife recording a video of *Love Found Me*, to standing on the historic Roseland Ballroom stage in New York City.

When my wife and I arrived in New York, I was dumbfounded. I had never been to New York and found the city amazing. They took us to Broadway shows, concerts, and other tours. We were treated like royalty for a long weekend. We ate great food, met great people and had the best time. We were supposed to meet Charlie Daniels and the band on Saturday afternoon to rehearse the song. When we arrived at the Roseland Ballroom, they were already practicing with other singers. Two bands were going to play songs for all the different acts, so they would not have to change out the stage and slow down the show.

The director asked me to come up on stage and get ready. After getting set up and being excited to see what it was like to play with a professional band, they informed me of a slight issue. The band had just been given the CD of my song when they got off the bus and had not had a chance to listen to it. They were already late for an appointment on a radio show and did not have time to work through it that afternoon.

"No problem!" the band said, "We will just meet you backstage and work on it tonight because we have an hour and a half before we go on to play." I was a little concerned, but the band seemed to be fine pushing it off, and Charlie Daniels said it would be fine. When Charlie Daniels says it will be fine, you go with it! Everyone left, and we went back to the hotel to get ready.

That night I remember going to the venue being super excited. I got backstage and had my own dressing room! Like so many things in life, the glamor that we see on TV is not reality. A white piece of paper was taped to the door with my name printed on it. It was a very, very small room. It reminded me of a study room at the local library back home. It had about four chairs, dirty carpet, and whitewashed walls. It could have been infested with roaches and I wouldn't have cared.

I kept waiting and waiting and waiting, and waiting, for Charlie and the band to show up. When I looked at my watch and realized we were about 30 minutes from going on stage, I began to worry. I thought they would probably cancel my song.

About that time Charlie Daniels knocked on my door and said "Hey man, our room is full. Can the band come in here with you?" No sooner did he ask than the entire band started streaming in and introducing themselves. We packed into that little room like sardines!

I looked around, noticed no one brought their instruments, and asked where we could practice. The drummer said, "We listened to your song a couple of times. I think we have it."

Charlie looked at me and said, "Pick up your guitar and play and sing the song for us." They listened and nodded.

After I had finished, Charlie gave me some instructions on how to start and end the song. He also said to speed it up a few beats because this was a live show. Always play a song a little faster when you play it live.

I played the song for the group again the way Charlie had described. They looked at each other and said, "That's it!" They told me to do it just like that again on stage, then they all stood up and walked out. The next time I saw them was when I was walking up on stage.

Charlie was standing with fiddle in hand behind me. The room was packed. My wife is a great singer and was able to be on stage to sing the female vocalist part. They introduced me on a huge video screen that showed the number of the contestant submissions, and then showed me and clips of my submission. They said, "Please welcome the winner of the contest here to perform his song . . ."

So, I stepped up to the mic and performed a song that had never been played in public, never practiced by a band, and never even sound checked. We all played the song, I sang my heart out, and without one practice, the song came off sounding like we were playing the CD. The band nailed it! The crowd loved it. I could not believe it. I had never seen or been a part of anything like that in my whole life. What started as a frustrating evening full of writer's block, ended a few months later as a truly amazing experience I will never forget. The special ingredient was clarity.

The contest opened a lot of doors for me, including the possibility of a music career. My wife and I traveled to Nashville many times over the following years to meet with Artists and Repertoire (A&R) reps, publishing companies, managers, and other industry professionals.

Ultimately, the contest presented me with a fork in the road. I had to decide if I wanted to dive into a career in music. Should I quit my job and move to Nashville? What would life look like in the music business? Could I write songs that were more commercial and less personal?

People outside of the industry don't realize that the music business is just that, a business. I learned that during my trips to Nashville. My wife would have to quit her job too. Was it worth it? *What would failure look like? What would success look like?*

A friend of mine, Lee Brice, began to make a name for himself in the industry about the same time. At the time he was not famous, but I knew he would be. I had played with him back in college, and we had many conversations about the opportunity to go and play in Nashville.

One day Lee left. Mid-spring of our junior year I went to his apartment and he was gone. I asked his roommate where he had gone and was told that Lee had left for Nashville. It was the middle of the semester, and he felt like he had the clarity he needed, so he packed up his things one night and was gone. I met up with Lee years later, and we both shared a laugh about that story. Lee knew what he wanted more than college, more than a girlfriend, and more than a job. He wanted to have a career in the music business.

Important decisions like the examples above require us to seek clarity. We seek clarity when we need understanding. In the midst of an issue or problem, clarity gives us understanding, discernment between options, builds our confidence, which helps us move forward.

We realize how important clarity is when we need to navigate the white spaces or when we need to move from where we are to where we want to be. Where do we start to close gaps and create movement? *Clarity.*

The Oxford Living Dictionary defines clarity as:

1. The quality of being *coherent* and *intelligible.*
2. The quality of being *easy to see* or hear; *sharpness of image* or sound.[4]

When we need clarity in our lives or businesses, we need to *develop a mental picture of something that makes sense, reflects reality and is easy to understand.* When we face difficult situations and difficult decisions, we work hard to find a solution that makes sense and is easy to understand. The more clarity we have, the sharper the picture we create.

Consider the problems I faced when deciding whether or not to change careers by going into the music industry. At first, I painted a picture of what life would look like in the music business. However, being in my mid-20's, that picture was full of desires, like living a life of performing in packed stadiums, traveling the world, making millions of dollars, and any other excess you could imagine.

Was the picture clear? YES! Was the picture coherent or did it accurately reflect my future reality? NO! But, why not? Well, it did not include all the rejections of my songs by music labels (like so many other performers had to overcome) or all the nights on a bus or in a van, or in a bar or hotel room away from friends and family. It did not include what my life would look like if I did not land a record or songwriting deal; or if I got a deal and failed to become a commercial success.

My picture was full of all the dreams and none of the realities.

How hard would it be to walk into the music business with expectations like the ones portrayed in my rosy picture? As soon as I encountered rejection or hard work, it would be devastating and potentially derail my movement. However, if I expected all those rejections, nights on the bus, and hard times, the likelihood of success would dramatically increase because my expectations would closely match my future reality.

> **The goal of clarity is to help us move from the *general* to the *specific*.**

There are three major steps when you want to move from the general to the specific.

1. List all the potential available alternatives or opportunities.
2. Collect all available data or information.
3. Think deeply about *what you want.*

Without realizing it, we go through this process every day before making decisions. So, the process isn't new; we just need to make purposeful choices about how and when to apply it to move from general, lower level decisions, to specific, highly intentional decisions. Stanford professor, Ronald Howard, boils the list down to three questions you can remember[5]:

1. What can I do? (alternatives, opportunities, response)
2. What do I know? (data, probability, risk)
3. What do I want? (Values, goals, intentions)

Chapter 2

Fuzzy Photos

Your vision will become clear only when you can look into your own heart. Who looks outside, dreams; who looks inside, awakes.

— Carl Jun

At the beginning of each of the four parts in this book, there are pictures of patents filed with the US Patent office long ago. Each one represents innovation, but also, and more importantly, people creating movement in their respective field. To download these images enhanced with important topics from the book, visit: **www. ThinkMoveThrive.com/resources**.

Pillar I is about clarity, the foundational building blocks of it, and how to better understand clarity. So, we begin with a sketch of a camera patented in the late 1800's, a fitting visual for creating clarity through pictures.

As we build clarity, our goal is to be able to answer general questions like: Do we jump into the music business or not? And to do that, we need an understanding of what we can see and what is missing in our pictures.

In response to these questions, we need to consider what we can see and what is missing in our picture. To take a picture, we need three things: light, focus, and filters.

1. Light exposes, enlightens, and gives a general idea of the picture.

2. Focus sharply defines the lines and boundaries of the picture.
3. Filters change the way we see the picture by enhancing or distorting the picture, depending on our "frame" of reference or type of frame we look through.

The picture below is missing all three elements.

Light

When we start with a problem, we begin to flesh out a general direction. To do that we need to take stock of all our available options. The picture above does not provide enough light. We can't tell if it is of an ocean, a sky, a city skyline, a group of people, or a person.

FUZZY PHOTOS

Light gives us a general theme.

When trying to gain clarity, we need to illuminate the big idea, as well as the opportunities and/or forks in the road we might encounter. By adding light, we can begin comparing the big differences.

When we ask questions to illuminate, they are about big, broad things. Our goal is to define all the options and alternatives, so we get a general idea of what is possible.

Light enlightens.

Like my 'ah-ha' moment writing a song, clarity can hit you as an enlightening moment. When I started writing the song, *Love Found Me*, I didn't have all the words in verses, but I did have a general direction of the song's message. A moment of clarity about that direction helped kick-start movement in my writing.

Experiencing a moment of clarity, when struggling with an addiction of any kind, may allow us to see the addiction for what it really is: a problem.

Light exposes.

In the introduction of the book, we talked about meditation techniques to improve a patient's ability to curb their addiction. These techniques allowed the person and the addiction to be exposed. Once exposed, we feel vulnerable and are forced to be honest about our situation. Too often addictions win the battle because the individual denies the destruction on the horizon rather than facing reality.

Imagine your problem involves several dark pictures. Without light, you've no way of knowing if they are related to each other, to you, or to future circumstances or consequences.

By adding a little light, we can get an idea of the general themes and attributes of each picture (or option) and begin making comparisons and developing decisions.

For example, we have a thick winter coat, but not a bathing suit. Light reveals the general theme of the pictures and we can decide to move toward those with snow instead of beaches.

When we struggle with addictive behaviors, light enlightens us and exposes our other options. If we become overwhelmed by our options or lack of options, we can add to our clarity by jotting down the facts we do know, such as: I am an addict. I need help to not be an addict. I have a job skill.

This is the beginning stage or infancy of clarity where we are attempting to generally clarify our situation with obvious facts, like 800-pound gorillas roaming around the room.

Now, check out the picture below. It is the same picture shown above, but with light added. What an amazing, top-of-the-world view of a mountain peak.

Of course, we can't look at it for very long because it tires our eyes. We can get a general idea from the image, but it lacks details that will allow us to further clarify the image.

Focus

Even though light reveals a general theme, it's not enough information to make decisions. We need to bring our pictures into focus. And to do that successfully, we need a lens to bring our pictures into focus. Our lens will be detailed facts that sharpen our comprehension of the problem and our options.

By collecting and assimilating detailed data, we begin to not only sharpen the picture, but to determine if the picture is accurate. Without focus, we cannot capture the reality of the photograph that light has exposed.

Once we define the picture and narrow our available options, we can clarify the direction of our decisions.

Using our music career decision example, we would start focusing on and adding new data and details gathered from many perspectives, such as: What is the cost of living in Nashville? Do we have sufficient savings? Do I need to get a part-time job? What local contacts and resources can be leveraged? What are the odds of 'making it'?

A meeting with a Universal A&R rep revealed that they sign five big acts a year. Each act receives one million dollars for marketing, touring, and growing their act. Only two of the five acts make it – meaning, they make enough to pay back the million-dollar investment and keep working.

Gathering information from managers, A&R reps, and friends like Lee Brice who was just breaking into the business – plus considering our financial position and our current jobs – helped us create a very clear picture of our potential life in Nashville. This way, we could have realistic expectations about our available options. Without all those added details, it would have been much harder to make a great decision and create positive movement.

> ✴ *Focus exposes inconsistencies in your scene.*

With focus, you begin to notice things in your problem picture that just don't make sense.

I am a big fan of Sesame Street. I remember watching Big Bird and Mr. Snuffleupagus every afternoon. One of the games they played on Sesame Street was called: *What doesn't belong?* The game involved showing pictures of a few things, and then you picked out which thing did not match the other things.

Another game I enjoyed playing involved two almost-identical pictures. The object was to find the differences between the two. Winning this game on first glance takes a lot of focus.

Focus exposes the little details that make a picture unique, separating it from all other pictures. Light tells us, in general, what we see: mountains. Focus defines the mountains, revealing snow and rock and other details.

Let's look again at the mountain picture and add some focus.

Now in focus, we can see that this is the mountain's summit and we can see several climbers. We can also see that the climbers are spread out along the rim of the mountain.

With the aid of focus, we can start asking questions about our new information. Have they made it to the summit, or are they preparing for that last push? Are they on oxygen? Who took this picture, and from where?

We can now gain a better understanding and have more clarity about the reality of their current situation. If the climbers were wearing astronaut suits, we would be questioning the accuracy of the picture because astronauts on a mountain doesn't make sense.

In your life, you may have general ideas of the direction you need to move, but you may also have varying interests or abilities. How do you narrow them? How do you focus?

The process of focusing may call for insights from other people in your life who know you well and can help you in narrowing your options and avoid being paralyzed by choices.

Frame

Finally, we construct the mental pictures of available options using our frame of reference, which is even more ambiguous and varied than the ideas of light and focus. However, it is a part of our reality and very important when working toward gaining clarity.

We all have experiences that shape who we are. We have different backgrounds and traditions, come from different societies, and have experienced different trials and triumphs. We are all unique! Which means each of us sees the world as only *we* can – through *our* frame. Just as Albert Einstein's theory of relativity describes how objects may look different to observers moving at different speeds; the way you see a particular situation may look completely different to someone with a different frame. When you think of the picture of the mountains, which of the following images capture what you see?

Some people would look at the picture and long to be on the summit. Other people would look at the picture and think the climbers were insane and took too much risk. When someone accuses you of seeing the glass "half empty" or "half full," they are pointing out how you frame the world. It can be more negative or positive, but it is unique to you.

Frames distort reality.

I have three young daughters. One day our neighbor's daughter and two of her cousins came over to visit.

One of the cousins had been adopted through a foster program. She was about the same age as my daughters and my neighbor's daughter. They all came over to play in the yard, on the playset, and pick flowers.

They were outside for hours and when it was getting dark, we invited the crew of six young ladies into the house for a spontaneous supper. My wife had cooked some extra chicken quesadillas, so there was plenty to go around.

I had been at work, so it was the first time I met our dinner guests. As I entered our home, I smelled the chicken cooking and made my way to the table. I politely introduced myself and intended to ask each girl her name. However, when the little girl who had been in foster care saw me, she immediately asked my wife if she could eat outside by herself. She never made eye contact with me, never told me her name, and never acknowledged I was in the room. She just grabbed her quesadilla, not even taking a plate, and left to eat outside by herself.

Later, after we had finished eating, I had to go outside to get some tools to finish up a project. When she heard me leave the house, she came back inside and joined the rest of the girls.

This little girl's frame of reference had created a very different picture of me than I would have expected. To her, I was a big man. Big men are dangerous and do bad things to helpless children. On the other hand, the other two girls met a man who was friendly and enjoyed chatting over quesadillas.

My wife and I talked about this poor girl's reaction to me and how sad we were for her. We couldn't help but wonder about the trauma she had obviously experienced and hoped that living in a stable family would allow her to overcome her emotional scars.

I could not imagine anyone causing that much pain to an innocent little being. That young girl could struggle her entire life trying to envision, to frame, men in a healthy way, all because of the trauma she had gone through as a child.

Frames are built into our being and determine how we see the picture that is presented to us. Is our glass half empty or half full? Depends on our frame. In business, it has been proven over and over that diverse teams perform at a higher level than teams made up of people who are more alike. Why would that be so?

One reason has to do with our *frame distortions*. When we view a situation, we will likely see it through our frame, which may or may not be close to reality. When a very diverse team works together, their numerous and different frames help to develop a view that more accurately aligns with reality. This diversity becomes like the lens that helps us focus, helping us gain better clarity and make better decisions for results that align with our original intent.

Diverse teams win because they are not one-dimensional in how they approach problems and develop solutions.

Frames enhance context.

My family used to go to a place called Ghost Town, which was designed to look like the main street of a wild west town. It was a theme park on the very top of a mountain, so visitors had to ride a chairlift or train up the mountain to get there.

As a young boy, I enjoyed watching the gunfight that "spontaneously" broke out in front of the saloon every morning around 10 am. One of the souvenirs we brought home from these trips was a picture of our whole family dressed up as cowboys in an old-time saloon.

The picture looked like it was taken in the 1800's, with a grainy, black-and-white, slightly faded look. Would this picture have been as compelling or conjured thoughts of the Wild West if it had been taken in full color? No way. It would have been cheesy, like the whole family was going to some strange western-themed Halloween party. Just like the grainy picture enhanced the western attire, our frames enhance the context of our reality.

If you are a fan of the Olympics and hear the words "Miracle on ice" you immediately flash back to an image of the USA team beating the Soviet Union in the 1980 Olympics. It was just a hockey game. Right?

The USA team was full of amateur hockey players facing some of the greatest professionals in the world representing the Soviet Union. Back home, the United States had been part of the global economic recession, and many people were having trouble getting by financially. Morale was low. The United States and the Soviet Union were still engaged in the Cold War.

If you are an American in the Northeast who has struggled to pay bills or put gas in the car, watching your team pull off one of the greatest upsets in history takes on new meaning. Inspiring and moving, it could give you hope in the resiliency of America. In reality, it *was* just a hockey game, but depending on your frame, it was often so much more.

Frames can change.

I love the story that Steven Covey tells in his book, *7 Habits of Highly Effective People*. It is a great illustration of how our frames can change in a moment of time. When he refers to a 'paradigm shift,' he is referring to his frame changing.

"I remember a mini-Paradigm Shift I experienced one Sunday morning on a subway in New York. People were sitting quietly – some reading newspapers, some lost in thought, some resting with their eyes closed. It was a calm, peaceful scene.

"Then suddenly, a man and his children entered the subway car. The children were so loud and rambunctious that instantly the whole climate changed.

"The man sat down next to me and closed his eyes, apparently oblivious to the situation. The children were yelling back and forth, throwing things, even grabbing people's papers. It was very disturbing. And yet, the man sitting next to me did nothing.

41

"It was difficult not to feel irritated. I could not believe that he could be so insensitive to let his children run wild like that and do nothing about it, taking no responsibility at all. It was easy to see that everyone else on the subway felt irritated, too.

"So finally, with what I felt was unusual patience and restraint, I turned to him and said, "Sir, your children are really disturbing a lot of people. I wonder if you couldn't control them a little more?"

"The man lifted his gaze as if to come to a consciousness of the situation for the first time and said softly, "Oh, you're right. I guess I should do something about it. We just came from the hospital where their mother died about an hour ago. I don't know what to think, and I guess they don't know how to handle it either."

"Can you imagine what I felt at that moment? My paradigm shifted. Suddenly I saw things differently, I felt differently, I behaved differently. My irritation vanished. I didn't have to worry about controlling my attitude or my behavior; my heart was filled with the man's pain. Feelings of sympathy and compassion flowed freely. "Your wife just died? Oh, I'm so sorry. Can you tell me about it? What can I do to help?" Everything changed in an instant.

"Many people experience a similar fundamental shift in thinking when they face a life-threatening crisis and suddenly see their priorities in a different light, or when they suddenly step into a new role, such as that of husband or wife, parent or grandparent, manager or leader.

"It becomes obvious that if we want to make relatively minor changes in our lives, we can perhaps appropriately focus on our attitudes and behaviors. But if we want to make significant, quantum change, we need to work on our basic paradigms."[6]

That story is so vivid, and we can all immediately relate to Steven's feelings. What changed? Nothing but the point of view – his frame. So now the kids are still acting out on the subway, but Steven feels very different after he gains a clear understanding of the situation.

His frame changes in a single moment on the subway. Occasionally, time and events and knowledge change our frames in an instant. Other times, they may change slowly, as small events and added knowledge are absorbed, but they **do** change. We can even choose to change our frames.

Frames can also be double-edged swords. They can give us the energy to move, but if too distorted, they can cause our movements to produce unintended results. Frames tap into that center of justice and injustice in our brain. What should and shouldn't be. Deep emotion comes out of our frame, affecting our decisions and energy to move. This makes becoming self-aware of frames and emotions very important when understanding how to create movement.

Let's take a look at the story of LEGOs that will help us understand clarity more fully.

LEGO's Clarity Conundrum

The LEGO Group was in trouble.

Located in Billund, Denmark, in huge red, yellow, and blue brick headquarters, LEGO is an iconic brand. The name comes from the Danish words *leg godt*, which means "play well."[7] The company was founded back in the 1930s by a Danish carpenter. In the late 1950s, it patented the stud-and-tube coupling system.

By the year 2000, the company had achieved notoriety as the fifth largest toy maker in the world. However, the company had lost some of the focus that had catapulted it forward for so many years. LEGO began posting one-million-dollar losses every day in 2004. The grandson of the founder stepped down as CEO and appointed a turnaround specialist, Jørgen Vig Knudstorp.

The LEGO Group had relied on consultants' insights and focus groups as the bedrock of new product innovation and company direction. The experts had convinced management that the problem was the "little bricks" and the solution was a big brand.

So, the company moved into action figures and video games. But, despite all the changes, in-house studies were producing results that made the LEGO future look bleak. They suggested that today's kids face a phenomenon called *time compression*, which was caused by parents micro-managing their children's activities to produce a desired or designer child. Hyper-schedule-driven families have "compressed" the amount of time kids have available just to sit and play.

If you are LEGO and create building bricks that require large amounts of time to assemble, this is not good news at all!

Thus, LEGO might be susceptible to the conventional wisdom of changing the product mix and expanding the brand to combat the decline of children's play time.

There were other problems, too. The company felt they had to compete with the instant gratification of plug-and-play toys. In the digital world, the level of playing experience was changing. Would anyone want to play with LEGOs anymore?

Building a massive ship or X-Wing Fighter out of small block takes time and patience. The result requires delayed gratification, which is contrary to the direction of the current cultural shifts.

Finally, management may have feared they were being categorized as toys for nerds. They wanted to be "cool" like all the other toys! The company had been making the same type of blocks for decades. Was LEGO risking becoming irrelevant if they did not expand the brand to encompass cooler toys that would provide the children instant gratification?

All the metrics, in-house studies, and feedback backed up the consultants' opinions that LEGO needed to move away from the block. Or did they?

LEGO was trying hard to sustain success. They constantly conducted focus groups with moms and kids to understand how they should develop new products. Focus groups are great, right? Companies should listen to customers to gain clarity, right?

Yes and no.

It is very advantageous for a company to focus on what its customers want. However, LEGO's focus groups were flawed and were providing the company false results which reinforced poor product development and the flawed strategy.

So, what was the flaw? The focus groups were conducted in false environments. Ten moms would sit in a focus group circle in a generic room and sometimes, would even become competitive with other moms during the focus group. In some groups there would also be pressure for certain moms to agree or disagree with the group.

Then the kids would be asked, "What do you think about this toy?" or "Is that toy cool?" and be allowed to respond.

It sounds like the system should have been good enough, but it ultimately failed miserably. LEGO was asking the focus groups the wrong questions and the answers were leading them down a path of financial ruin.

The false environments LEGO created for moms and kids produced answers related to those environments. The answers would have changed, and more importantly, the questions would have changed if LEGO had created more realistic environments.

LEGO faced a decision: do we branch out away from blocks or dive deeper into blocks? It looked like the market was changing. That families had changed. That what people looked for in LEGOs was changing. It would be so tempting to throw in the towel and say, "we must change with the times."

However, that is not what happened at LEGO.

The CEO Knudstorp decided the company did not have true clarity. Instead of changing the organizational structure and product mix of the company, *he changed the focus of the company.*

He felt that the company, despite all the focus groups, had lost its connection to the customer base.

So, he *changed the questions*. Instead of asking "What toys do kids want?" he began asking "What is the role of play?" The shift in questions changed the way the company approached the relationship with their customers and how they connected with children.

LEGO trained teams of researchers to embed in people's homes to watch families all over the world play. They spent time with children on the floor, instead of bringing moms and kids into focus groups.

They interviewed everyone, took pictures, and produced photo diaries. They not only collected data about LEGO, but they also collected data about how families play. They brought all that data back to LEGO where it was painstakingly reviewed. Each researcher would pore over the information, looking for patterns.

So, what did they find out?

1. There was a link between nostalgia and the types of toys kids play with. For example, parents would say, "I remember playing with LEGOs as a kid, so I bought them for my kids."

2. Kids are suffocating under the management oversight of their parents. When asked to design their perfect room, they included booby traps and secret doors to hide things. They needed to find free air away from their parents just to play. Boys also enjoyed using play to infuse a little danger into a "bubble wrapped" life.

3. Boys used play to form hierarchies. Video games, basketball scores, or any type of play would be used to establish alpha/beta standings or other types of social orders.

4. Kids used play to demonstrate mastery. A skateboarder's prized possession was his old shoes that had all the scars from the falls he had taken to become a great skater.

5. The average kid does not have time to play with LEGOs. However, digging into the data showed that while many children did not have time to play with LEGOs, 40% had plenty of time. That is a lot of kids! Understanding the data in more detail exposed a fact that did not initially surface: the market potential for the little blocks was still massive.

The new findings produced something that was extremely valuable to LEGO: *clarity*. For the first time, they understood the act of children playing, why they play, what they gain from play, and how much time kids have to play. The understanding gained from not only their customers, but also their non-customers, helped them form a very comprehensive view of the reality of play of kids around the world.

So, why does all that matter? At this point, LEGO knows how kids play, but continues to lose money.

> **Clarity is only useful when it is used to give direction and intentionality to movement. Clarity is not actually moving.**

LEGO could know the psychology of kid's play at an intimate level, but without acting, it would be worthless to them. We need clarity so that we can move with *intent* when we execute. So, how did LEGO create movement?

They increased outreach to a community called Adult Fans of LEGO (AFOL). They sent representatives to AFOL conventions – yes, there is such a thing as a LEGO convention for adults – who tapped into the community for product ideas and feedback.

Then, they started producing products with a covert sense of danger, like a fire truck for boys. Next, they would "secretly" release plans on the internet to be able to transform the firetruck into a toy weapon or other adventuresome items.

They launched the LEGO clubhouse where kids could come and build LEGOs in a retail environment.

In the clubhouse, there are different skill levels of LEGOs to allow informal mentorship and networking based on a hierarchy of skill. Younger kids could learn from older kids. Understanding play and what motivates kids gave the company valuable information on which product lines were valuable and which were not. They reduced the product lines from 12,000 to 7,000.

And lastly, they changed the company motto to "Inspiring the Builders of Tomorrow," which established a stronger sense of purpose. The new motto is bold, simple, and inspiring. The new direction of the company is fun and meaningful. The big question is: did it work?

In their last financial report available on their website, sales were up over 25% in 2015 with earnings of over 1.3 billion dollars.[8] A decade after the journey to clarity began one of the highest-grossing LEGO sets sold in 2015 was the LEGO Star Wars™.

The insights LEGO gained from understanding why kids play continues to produce outstanding returns and further proves that LEGO's clarity on play was accurate. The picture of reality they constructed, and their response and alignment to that reality, took the company **from losing a million dollars a day to profits of over 3 million dollars a day**.

In the LEGO story, we uncovered some pitfalls that can happen when we lack clarity. We learned how hard it can be to construct clarity. And finally, how valuable clarity is when you get it right.

LEGO had a big decision on whether to branch out or double down on the blocks. They needed to move from the general to the specific. They started by asking better questions, which allowed them the clarity to see where LEGO "fit" into how kids play. The focus gained from understanding how kids play helped create a clear path forward.

We have seen how light (asking the right question) and focus (building toys with an element of danger) gave LEGO clarity, but how did their frames affect their clarity?

Earlier, we discovered that the LEGO executives thought that their blocks were being categorized as "toys for nerds." If you were afraid that was the popular stigma of your company what would you do? Find ways to become cool!

We can understand the logic behind some of the decisions that LEGO made. However, the frames they were using seemed to be emanating out of a place of fear. The fear of becoming irrelevant or the fear of their blocks going out of style. The problem became that the frame distorted the actual reality.

It wasn't until the CEO asked the question: "How do kids use play?" that he started to change the perspective (frame) of how he saw the LEGO blocks. The CEO gained clarity. Clarity is more than data. Clarity is more than feedback.

> **Clarity is seeing reality as it really is and using that to build your future movement toward what you want.**

Clarity involves understanding data and emotions. It calls for the seeker to understand the difference between the intentions and the results. *Seeing the gaps.* Seeing warts, problems, challenges. Understanding the true opportunity. What is real? What is true reality?

Clarity almost sounds overwhelming, because we know that no two individuals can see reality the same way. Is it possible to construct a perfectly clear reality?

Yes, but not on our own. We need to involve others because we are finite – and others bring diversity of perspectives which give us greater focus and clearer view of reality.

The light and focus over time helped change the frame, which helped LEGO simplify their approach and bring the company back from the brink of financial disaster.

We have reviewed what I believe are the building blocks of clarity. And we have studied how they fit together in the LEGO story.

Let's dive deeper into how to create clarity. If clarity is made up of light, focus, and frames, we need a step-by-step process to find the light, etch the focus, and develop healthy, flexible frames.

LEGO was intentional about how they cultivated clarity. We can use some of the same methods and take simple steps to cultivate clarity in our lives and businesses.

Chapter 3

Cultivating Clarity

Some persons are very decisive when it comes to avoiding decisions.
— Brendan Francis

Wouldn't it be great if we could gain clarity in life as easily as snapping a Polaroid™ picture? If we could have a camera in our mind's eye and just point and click? And then, magically, a picture would roll from our brains, a visualization of perfect clarity in crystal detail. Unfortunately, clarity is more complex and develops over time. Even when we have an "ah-ha" moment, we still need to fill in the details to generate a *Living Visual*. A Living Visual is your mental visualization of what you want to create in the future. It is "Living" because as we will see in this chapter, it can change over time. "Visual" is short for visualization because we create the image in our minds eye and then set our course towards making it reality.

Many times, we wrestle with problems, decisions, or future directions, putting maximum effort towards building our Living Visual. Like a farmer with an empty field, putting in the time and energy to plan for producing a harvest. The farmer cultivates his desired crop by considering and choosing the fertilizers and soil adjustments necessary for success. Like the farmer, we can cultivate clarity.

When we attempt to begin cultivating clarity, moving from the general picture to a more defined and detailed picture, we can use seven important and powerful tactics. These tactics cover specific elements we need to identify in our problem, so we can make decisions and solidify our snapshot of clarity.

To gain the most accurate reality, based on the greatest clarity, we need to use as many of the seven tactics as possible.

The more tactics we include in our cultivation of clarity, the greater the likelihood that the result will match our expectations and intent.

Let's take a look at the seven *Cultivating Clarity Tactics*.

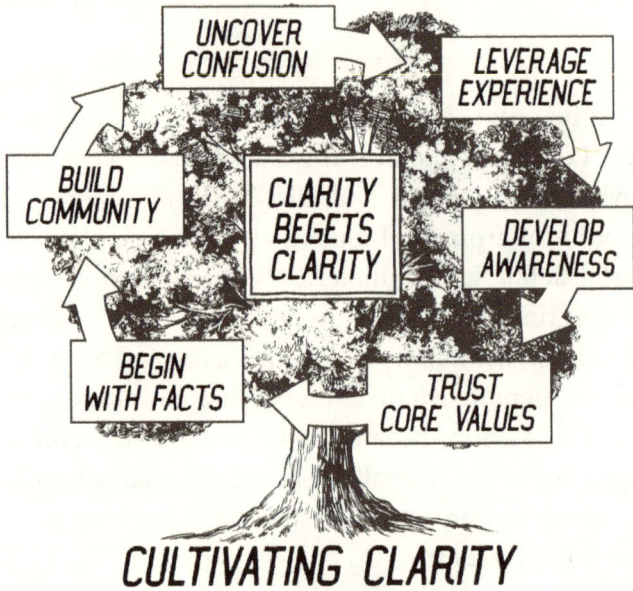

UNCOVER CONFUSION

LEVERAGE EXPERIENCE

BUILD COMMUNITY

CLARITY BEGETS CLARITY

DEVELOP AWARENESS

BEGIN WITH FACTS

TRUST CORE VALUES

CULTIVATING CLARITY
fig. 2

We will cover each of the seven tactics in detail and how they will aid you in generating clarity.

1 Uncover Confusion

I learned about the value of confusion in my high school chemistry class, oddly enough, where a solitary poster of an orangutan stared out at the class, with the quote at the bottom:

> *"I know you think you understand what you thought I said, but I'm not sure you realize that what you heard is not what I meant."*

The classroom held around twenty desks, the ones with the wood top and plastic seats in bright primary colors. The teacher's desk, with a lab table beside it, sat at the front of the room. Both were usually covered in a mess of papers, a grade book, narrow blank Scantron® test papers (if you are too young to know, look it up) and a random assortment of objects ranging from student projects to lab experiments.

The most important spot in the room, however, was the enormous lab table drawer that was cram-packed with stacks and stacks of Laffy Taffy wrappers, bundled together like playing cards. No taffy — just wrappers. Why were there Laffy Taffy wrappers in my chemistry class . . . and why were they important? A little backstory will help with the answer.

My high school was in rural South Carolina with about 800 students. It was small enough where you could know just about everyone in the school, at least generally. It was also small enough to have only one chemistry teacher.

Every day, that teacher would come into class after the bell rang, sit down at his desk, and ask the class about their homework from the day before. Sometimes he would take up the homework and sometimes he wouldn't. You never knew which he was going to do.

Other times, he would make the class trade homework assignments and grade each other's papers. This made for a very friendly class with absolutely no bullies! You always hoped that the person grading your paper would be kind and give you grace, especially on days when the assignments were tough.

Before the class jumped into new material, the teacher would go to the lab table, reach into the drawer, and pull out some wrappers. Then he would start reading some of the corniest and most terrible jokes ever uttered. Just in case you aren't familiar with Laffy Taffy, each taffy wrapper had at least two awful jokes on the inside. The more jokes the teacher read, the more time it took from the chemistry lesson. I had never witnessed students working so relentlessly to stuff Laffy Taffy wrappers into the drawer just to get out of five minutes of chemistry class!

Once the jokes were read, the wrappers were rubber-banded together again and thrown to the back of the drawer. After guessing the answers to the terrible, horrible, no-good, very bad jokes, it was time to learn.

The teacher would take the time to cover the concept verbally, have students read the concept aloud from their textbooks, and many times draw the concept on the board. He would then assign some problems to work on during class. While the class struggled to figure out the problems, the teacher would stand at the front of the class and swing a yardstick like a baseball bat.

Inevitably, someone would yell "It's impossible!" and the teacher would ask that someone, "What is wrong?" The frustrated student would always blurt something like, "I will never get this! I am so confused!"

This was when the show would start.

The teacher would jump into the air (already standing 6'4") and yell, "That's GREAT! Confusion is a GOOD THING!"

And then, the whole class would chime in: "We are all confused!"

He would keep repeating how great being confused was until the class was in an uproar and finally asked the right question: Why was confusion so good?

He had the class right where he wanted them, as he would explain and constantly repeat: *if you are confused, you are using your noodle.*

Confusion forces you to think. It makes you step out of your comfort zone or change the way you look at things to discover something you don't currently understand.

The students would go through and describe all the things they did not know. Eventually, someone would figure out a part of the problem and start sharing it with the rest of the class. Before long, everyone was working together, learning together, and developing one of the first major skills in creating clarity.

> To develop or create clarity, the journey must start from a place without clarity. We call that place confusion.

Chemistry class was always an adventure, and an experience I'll never forget.

Another reason I won't forget the class is that my dad was the teacher. He was known to the students as Dad Burnett, and they thought his class was awesome.

In high school, it's tough generating positive responses from students in chemistry class, but I watched my dad use humor to help us all overcome the frustration that comes with learning something new.

I learned a lot about chemistry in that class, but the most valuable thing I learned was the life skill of developing clarity by recognizing, and even promoting, a state of confusion.

~~~~

How long has it been since you have been confused or perplexed? When has something shaken you out of your daily rhythm and made you start asking some difficult questions?

Clarity is not for people who already know it all. They have something much easier: blind ignorance and pride.

Confusion is the first step down the path to clarity, because it forces us to change our approach, step outside our comfort zone, look at reality from a different angle, and ask better questions.

You arrive a place of confusion by taking risks, pushing to a new level, exposing more of who you are and who you are not. Confusion can also be manifested by external or internal forces that affect our lives. Either way, if something has changed or needs to change and you lack clarity, the best place to start is from a place of confusion, where your mind is open.

If you are confused, don't be embarrassed! There is no shame in it. Confusion is a good thing and is the first step to greater clarity. Just take the initiative to move from confusion to clarity.

Ask great questions, try new approaches, and take risks.

Leverage Experience

Clarity can be formed by experiencing new situations. Our brain is an amazing instrument that automatically records, organizes, and makes sense of our experiences to help us expedite future decisions. It also forms patterns and prototypes, which we use to expedite our decision process.

This is handy, because if we had to consider every possibility of every situation, we might never get out of bed in the morning. Our brains take prioritized information from experiences, combines it with tried-and-true patterns (egg dropped in a hot skillet cooks – egg dropped on the floor splatters = watch where you drop an egg), so we can make better decisions faster.

The book, *Sources of Power*, deals exclusively with how people make decisions. The book covers many examples of how experience shapes our decision making.

One great example of experience helping to cultivate clarity is demonstrated in how first responders and firefighters deal with emergencies.

Consider the following examples from *Sources of Power*:[9]

The Laundry Chute Fire

The initial report is of flames in the basement of a four-story apart-ment building: a one-alarm fire. The commander arrives quickly and does not see anything. There are no signs of smoke anywhere. He finds the door to the basement, around the side of the building, enters, and sees flames spreading up the laundry chute. That's simple: a vertical fire that will spread straight up. Since there are no external signs of smoke, it must be just starting.

The way to fight a vertical fire is to get above it and spray water down, so he sends one crew up to the first floor and another to the second floor. Both report that the fire has gotten past them.

The commander goes outside and walks around to the front of the building. Now he can see smoke coming out from under the eaves of the roof.

It is obvious what has happened: the fire has gone straight up to the fourth floor, has hit the ceiling there, and is pushing smoke down the hall.

Since there was no smoke when he arrived just a minute earlier, this must have just happened. It is obvious to him how to proceed now that the chance to put out the fire is quickly gone. He needs to switch to search and rescue, to get everyone out of the building, and he calls in a second alarm.

The side staircase near the laundry chute has been the focus of activity before. Now the attention shifts to the front stairway as the evacuation route.

In this situation, the commander's experience helped build a mental prototype of the situation so that he "automatically" knew his initial course of action, while continuing to gather new data.

His experience gave him great clarity during a stressful situation and kept him from needing extra time to weigh options before executing the path forward. His superior experience, combined with assimilating new data, was like having wisdom on autopilot.

It may seem like we don't really think in these situations and just react; however, we can control *how* we react to external and internal forces.

And this is where leaning on our experience comes in, shortening the time it takes to process all the data, sometimes dramatically so. The more experience and awareness we have in the moment, the faster we can generate clarity on how to react.

Experience reduces the time necessary for gaining clarity.

Consider when you are struggling to find clarity with an issue. Part of your difficulty may be that you lack experience in solving that particular issue.

Fortunately, if your lack of experience is holding you back, you can supplement your experience short-fall with that of an expert in the field. With this added experience, you can quickly gain clarity and find solutions to your problem.

In business we often pay advisors, consultants, experts and coaches to help us compress the time it takes to solve a problem or create movement. It is possible to perform the task ourselves, but experience takes time.

One thing to always keep in mind is that even when enlisting the support of an expert, you need to continue to gather data about the problem, so your resulting clarity reflects the most current status of the problem (the fire racing to the roof).

Experience paired with relevant, timely data dramatically improves clarity.

When we lean on experience, we can also benefit from noticing subtle details. If someone asked me to judge a dance competition, most of the contestants would get a score of 9 or 10. The reason being that I have no experience, so everyone (unless they dance as badly as I do) would look the same to me. However, ask a classically trained ballerina, with 10 years of dance experience in New York to judge the same competition, and the scores would more accurately reflect the skill of the dancer. Why? The ballerina sees the subtle clues and details that a non-professional dancer misses.

Experience makes data more meaningful.

The example below describes another situation in a burning building. Notice how the firefighter uses experience to discern between available options.

The Sixth Sense

It was a simple house fire in a one-story house in a residential neighborhood. The fire is in the back, in the kitchen area. The lieutenant leads his hose crew into the building toward the back to spray water on the fire, but the fire just roars back at them.

"Odd," he thinks. The water should have more of an impact. They try dousing it again, and get the same results. They retreat a few steps to regroup. Then the lieutenant starts to feel as if something is not right. He doesn't have any clues; he just doesn't feel right about being in that house, so he orders his men out of the building – a perfectly standard building with nothing out of the ordinary.

As soon as his men leave the building, the floor where they had been standing collapses. Had they still been inside, they would have plunged into the fire below.

Onlookers would have watched the firefighters exit and mistakenly exclaimed how lucky they were to get out just in time. However, the lieutenant was not so much lucky as he was aware. It was his *sixth sense* or intuition that gave him insight into a situation that did not make rational sense but saved the lives of his team.

Unlike the laundry chute fire example, this lieutenant did not have enough data to know exactly what was going to happen, but his experience was deep enough to set off his '*Spidey'* sense.

Experience not only offers clarity as we move forward, but also gives us insight into areas where we may face unknown catastrophe.

Experience can help us mitigate or eliminate loss.

This idea of the importance of experience in finding clarity may sound discouraging if you are a teenager, just graduating college, or starting your first job.

I remember being extremely discouraged leaving an interview with a business owner when I was in my twenties. He had just told me very candidly that my resume matched every single qualification he was looking for, but he couldn't hire me for the job. When I asked for his reason, he said, "I am looking for someone with more gray hair."

That was a pretty devastating answer for a twenty-four-year-old looking for his next challenge. There was nothing I could do, short of aging twenty years, to meet the bar he had set. Even though the business owner could have chosen his words more wisely, what he meant was that he most valued an applicant's experience.

What if we don't have a lot of experience with a particular situation or job? Rely heavily on the other clarity-generating tactics. Gather as much information as you can on the subject in which you lack experience.

Speed up or enrich your experience by feeding your brain with stories of another person's experience. While not as powerful as the experience itself, knowledge based on others' experiences can still help your brain become acclimated to the subject and begin building models and patterns.

Finally, find a mentor, coach, consultant, expert, or wise advisor with the experience you are seeking, who is willing to offer you counsel. As we grow, develop, take risks, and create movement, we learn and earn the value of experience.

Develop Awareness

Let's reconsider the example of the lieutenant, who saved his team's life by telling them to evacuate the burning building.

We have discussed how experience helped him know that something wasn't right, and how his "ah-ha" moment came when he connected the dots between his past experience and the present situation. He drew from his experience in the context of the present situation to help form a clearer picture of the true reality. He knew his options and the potential threat of the environment. He was using all his senses and his instinct, which resulted in becoming very *aware* of the precarious situation.

> *When we heighten our awareness, we start to pay attention to details we normally miss.*

When I was a boy, I would explore the fields and woods around my home. Occasionally, I would find arrowheads that were remnants of the Native American tribes that lived in our area hundreds of years earlier.

At the time, for me, these arrowheads were treasures! Some were meticulously carved and would transport me into an imaginary world, where I would imagine being a Native American Indian, hunting wild animals to feed and clothe my family.

When a real Native American Indian went out to hunt birds or deer, he heightened his awareness. He became quiet. He shifted his focus to hear the smallest sounds. He sharpened his vision to see hidden details in the landscape, looking for signs that would lead him to his prize. And when he finally found the wild animal and pulled back his bow, he would pay attention to his breathing, so it would not affect the trajectory of his arrow.

Awareness is intentional. It is deliberate. It takes effort to create and develop. When we have keen awareness, it helps enhance our experience and can expose patterns in the available data that may have been missed. It helps us to better understand our strengths and weaknesses.

> If you want to know the role you play in your work, relationships, and parenting, you need to become more self-aware.

Awareness does not occur by accident. We have to desire and seek awareness for it to develop. Awareness is both internal and external.

Just like the hunter, we choose to heighten our environmental awareness to see our Living Visual in more detail.

Like the hunter intentionally controlling his breathing, our internal or self-awareness can help us control our responses more effectively. How do you deal with anger? Do you become verbally aggressive? How do you deal with criticism? Do you internalize it?

Becoming more *self*-aware gives you the power to recognize your tendencies, and tools to help you mitigate the negative effects. Here are four methods we can use to significantly and intentionally develop our awareness: **Meditation, Reflection, Visualization,** and **Prayer.**

~ Meditation ~

As we develop awareness a valuable tool that can give tremendous clarity is meditation. The word meditation can take on different meanings, but in this book, it means focusing the mind or thinking deeply on a specific idea. For example, we may choose to think on the idea of forgiveness. We may think about the idea of forgiveness from many angles and meditate on what it means to us. What does it mean religiously? What does it mean practically? What does it do for me psychologically? We may ask questions like who we need to forgive or who we need to ask for forgiveness.

We may also practice a "now present" type of meditation commonly known as mindfulness. One objective of mindfulness meditation is NOT to think about anything, but instead, focus our minds on the present moment.

In my early 30s, I was working, going to grad school at night, and my wife and I had our first daughter. I started having difficulty sleeping and was experiencing bouts of anxiety. I had come to a place where I could not turn my mind off, even though I was exhausted and desperately needed sleep. Problems from the past were dragging me down and worries about the future were keeping me up at night.

What I needed was a quiet space in my head to work on what was right in front of me.

Meditation helped me regain control of my mind and create the quiet space I needed. With practice, I found that I could clear my mind and focus on the present moment.

Instead of letting marketing ads, negative news, our online social community, and other people dictate the direction of our thinking, meditation gives us the power to take control of our thoughts. And when we intentionally take control of our thoughts, we start to see what types of thoughts are holding us back or pushing us ahead.

With a clutter-free mind, we can better take in the details that immediately affect us. We are able to become aware of and to hear our instincts and convert that awareness and insight into meaningful action.

How often do you intentionally practice clearing your mind to focus on the work of the day?

~ Reflection ~

Let's stop a moment here. Now, remember a time in your life when you were extremely content. Got it? Next, ask yourself: *why* were you content?

The idea of reflection is not "living in the past" or internalizing past failures, but rather is taking a situation in the past and evaluating it from multiple points of view. As we develop awareness in our lives, reflection gives us space to step back and look at past successes, failures, challenges, and opportunities that have led us to the present moment.

Healthy, pro-active reflection allows us the space needed to step out of the emotions of the past and become an outside observer of a situation. Reflection helps expose flaws and strengths we may miss in the moment.

We can ask important questions, like: "Why did it bother me so much when he said . . .?" or "Why do I seem to always _____ whenever I am _____?"

When we think back to a situation that is related to our present situation, it can help give us light and focus. It can also help us adjust our current frames.

In high school, I read a Persian proverb that has always motivated me to reflect.

Men are four:
He who knows not and knows not he knows not,
he is a fool—shun him;
He who knows not and knows he knows not,
he is simple—teach him;
He who knows and knows not he knows,
he is asleep—wake him;
He who knows and knows he knows,
he is wise—follow him![10]

Reflecting sharpens our mental clarity by helping us refine and process our experiences and desires.

Experience is great, but worthless if you never learn from it. Reflection offers a path to learning. Desires are great, but reflection can help us determine if our desires are healthy or harmful.

The more we reflect, the more aspects of our past can help to sharpen the clarity we need in the present. The goal, when looking back, is to find information that helps us move. If we find ourselves looking back and becoming depressed or internalizing, we can paralyze our movement!

Don't give your past power over your future movements. Healthy reflection empowers your next step.

Let's admit that sometimes we tell ourselves inaccurate circumstances about a problem. We didn't get that promotion at work, because "they don't know all the work I do every day." She won't go out on a date with me, because "I don't have a new car." I can't start a business, because "I don't have any money."

When we reflect, we should start by running a self-check to discover if our response to certain situations or people is inaccurate and holding us back.

If we are wise, we realize that where we are in life is, in large part, due to our responses to decisions we have faced throughout our lives. That means we have something we can change.

With reflection, I could see that I have a temper at times. This admission may help me realize that a big reason I didn't get the promotion is because my employer doesn't trust me to be reasonable with customers.

What if reflection allowed me to see that I didn't have self-confidence? The young lady may not be going on a date with me simply because I haven't asked.

What if clarity from reflection revealed that I don't need money to start my business? Many investors would love to get involved in a startup business. If they haven't invested in mine, what do they see in me that keeps them from investing?

These are simple scenarios that expose the value of reflection.

Take time to dig a bit below the surface of circumstances you feel are holding you back. Find a safe place to work through tough questions about who you are and who you want to be. Many of our problems are solved by making small changes in how we view ourselves and our situations.

Remember Mahatma Gandhi's quote: "Be the change you wish to see in the world." Start by looking inward, then respond and move.

~ Visualization ~

Reflection forces us to process information and establish its context in the present.

In contrast, visualization uses information as context to build a visual picture of something not yet realized or understood. It may sound counter-intuitive, but part of developing awareness in the present requires the visualization of our future.

Visualization helps our brains simplify our lives by creating working pictures. We take the information we have and create something we can understand. We may be constructing a future state or trying to understand a current phenomenon.

Steve Jobs could see a future where people carried their entire music library in their pocket.

In the 1990s, the technology did not exist. His visualization helped him design the first iPod. Jobs visualized a future person, and then designed a product to meet their needs. Visualization is a skill that many great leaders have in common. If you want to lead, you must be skillful at building and describing the pictures of where your team is going.

You may be tempted to think that since you are not CEO of a Fortune 500 company, you don't need visualization. Not true!

Take five minutes and paint a picture of what you want your life to look like in three years. Are you in less debt? New job? Married? Kids?

Visualize what it is that you want to move toward. Create a picture in your mind that stirs positive emotion. Create a picture that you can be excited about moving towards.

Remember, execution requires energy. If you can see clearly what you want, you will gain energy from the visualization.

So many times, we miss opportunities because we don't take time to describe and understand what we really want in life.

In the Harvard Business Review, they describe how Boeing, an aerospace company, must visualize data.

"At Boeing, the managers of the Osprey program need to improve the efficiency of the aircraft's takeoffs and landings. But each time the Osprey gets off the ground or touches back down, its sensors create a terabyte of data. Ten takeoffs and landings produce as much data as is held in the Library of Congress. Without visualization, detecting the inefficiencies hidden in the patterns and anomalies of that data would be an impossible slog."[11]

Could you imagine, making sense of all the data in the Library of Congress!

Taking relevant data from an airplane landing, or our personal lives, helps us speed up meaningful movements. If we can't build a visualization from our life's data, we risk suffering from "analysis paralysis," meaning we analyze data for so long that we never actually do anything.

I remember the movie, *The Greatest Game Ever Played*, where an amateur goes up against two professional golfers. In one of the scenes, the professional golfer steps up to the tee, but before hitting the ball, he looks down the course at the hole. Suddenly, all the people start to melt away, and then the trees start to disappear. Finally, the sound dies down, and all that is left is the golfer standing on the tee box, looking out over a peaceful green pasture, blue skies above and the lonely flag on the horizon.[12]

The golfer mentally constructed a picture of the golf course filled with the important data, like the contour of the land, the golf ball and the distance to the flag, while leaving out data that cluttered the scene. This visualization process helped him focus and relax, right before smashing the ball down the center of the fairway.

Visualization is a powerful input into our development of awareness.

~ Prayer ~

When we pray, we open our minds and hearts up to something we believe is greater than ourselves.

We may pray for help when we are grieved, heartbroken, lost, lonely, or depressed. We may offer prayers of gratitude when we win, find love, receive a gift, or see beauty. We also can pray out of a sense of awe and thanksgiving. Regardless of when we pray, it forces us to see things from a new perspective and that new perspective increases our awareness.

We also may verbalize (even silently) needs, thoughts, desires or a wish that we would otherwise suppress or not openly communicate. Prayer is deeply personal.

Why does prayer lead to greater awareness?

When we pray, we're tapping into something that is more than physical and deeper than ordinary emotion. It is spiritual. When we express ourselves on a spiritual level, we grow in our awareness of the physical and emotional, too.

Scientific studies have shown prayer increases self-control and can build trust and unity between two people, along with many other well-being benefits.

We are spiritual beings. Part of awareness comes from being aware of not only our physical and emotional needs, but how they are also woven into the fabric of our lives with our spiritual needs.

When we pray, we exert energy to become aware on a spiritual level. Sometimes prayer can expose areas in our life that are empty or full. We may not even realize it until we hear ourselves say it.

When you speak something out loud, it can enlighten. *Words matter*.

Have you ever met someone who thinks while they speak? They may talk in what seems like circles, but they are fleshing out what they believe while they say it. It can sometimes be confusing for the listener because they may cover three different points of view, and then settle on one before the end of the conversation.

When we pray, we are working out what is in our hearts and minds, in our spirit. We are communicating those ideas and emotions not only to a higher power, but to ourselves. Exposing the needs of our spirit, heart, and mind builds our self-awareness.

Trust Core Values

It is funny to me when I visit companies that have fifteen core values posters plastered on the walls. It is almost like they got on a search engine, entered "great company values," and then regurgitated the list onto their walls.

Core values drive our actions.

"Core" means those few things that are embedded so deep in our hearts and lives that they could not be changed unless we changed our identity.

"Values" are those deeply held convictions that are so apparent and clear to us that they drive our behavior. They are our operating system running in the background. They can help give us bearings and direction in life during times of uncertainty. Having a strong and clear understanding of core values can also help us be more decisive.

I once toured one of Amazon's huge distribution centers with a local community non-profit organization.

At first glance, it was hard not to be amazed at the scope and organization of the operation, but by the time I left, I was more impressed with the core values that were embodied by the employees.

Our group stood on a mezzanine overlooking rows and rows of shelves packed full of consumer products. It was larger than ten football fields under one roof. All the people looked like they were busy bees going from place to place sorting and loading packages.

While we were taking in the sights, the tour guide told us a story.

She began by saying, "Here at Amazon, we do whatever it takes to get the item delivered on time."

She went on to tell about a mother and her young son, who was fighting cancer and would have to celebrate Christmas in the hospital. He had told his Mom that his one Christmas wish was for a purple ukulele. She ordered the ukulele online, well before Christmas, to ensure he received his Christmas wish on time. But then, a terrible ice storm shut down ground and air travel, and the ukulele couldn't be delivered by Christmas Day.

The boy's desperate mother called Amazon customer service looking for help. It was Christmas Eve.

Another purple ukulele was immediately located, in the same distribution warehouse we were touring, and customer service contacted the plant manager, explaining the situation. This warehouse just happened to be in the same city as the hospital where the young boy and his mother awaited Christmas.

Amazon warehouses are closed one day a year, Christmas Day.

But on this Christmas Day, the plant manager and one of his assistant managers came to the closed Amazon distribution center and located the purple ukulele among the football fields of products. The plant manager then drove to the hospital to hand-deliver that little boy's one Christmas wish.

That story of dedication and commitment to core values permeated the culture of that facility so deeply that the amateur tour guide wanted to share it with strangers on a mezzanine. She believed in that core value, put energy towards accomplishing it and could communicate it powerfully with one simple story.

Do the employees at that Amazon distribution facility have to be reminded of core values by some wall poster declaring: "We deliver packages on time"? No way!

Core values produce clarity because they are what we believe to be true and right. This is a wellspring of energy we need when our execution and movement become difficult and we ask if it's all worth it. The deeper and more aligned our activities are with things we care about, the greater the energy and patience we will produce to carry us across the finish line.

Begin with Facts

In around 387 BC, the fragile city of Rome was invaded by a powerful army led by Brennus, Gaelic warlord and chieftain, that annihilated the weaker Roman army. For years, Rome had been ruled by the Etruscans, who had left the city with poor defenses.

Legend has it that the surviving citizens barricaded themselves on the Capitoline Hill, but it was a futile effort, and the Romans were beaten.

To add insult to injury, Brennus forced the Romans to pay him and his Gaelic warriors 1,000 pounds of gold to leave Rome.

The loss to Brennus and the Gauls left a deep mark on the Romans. Determined never to allow the same destruction to happen again, the Romans studied their defeat and revamped their entire army from what they learned.

Greater emphasis was placed on building a strong army and developing the weapons technology they had encountered in battle, such as more advanced iron-working techniques, weapons designed for close-quarter combat, as well as full-body shields.

The larger shields had been used in a way never before seen, being held so they overlapped edge-to-edge, forming an impenetrable "turtle" shell the Roman attackers could not penetrate.

The Romans also erected a large defensive wall to improve city fortifications. And finally, they altered their battle line strategy to include special placement of their more experienced and wealthier soldiers, a group known as the Triarii.[13]

The Romans didn't just get angry at the Gauls – they got better.

When we *Begin with Facts*, we add something specific to our Living Visual: Contrast. The details we see make the lines in our picture stand out with greater sharpness. We begin to see differences that we could not distinguish before.

For Rome, it took looking at why the enemy was able to beat them to begin the process of becoming the best army.

What facts are you overlooking that can add focus to your Living Visual? What do you know right now that can help you move?

When we study what makes the great performers, athletes, businessmen, parents, or students execute at the highest level, we find that they are able to see things other people don't see and incorporate those insights into their execution. They are great at seeing, managing, and improving the little details.

For example, take major league baseball players. There is one physical attribute all hitting baseball players in the major league share that is better than other players in the minors, college or even high school.

It isn't speed or strength – nope, Major league baseball hitters have unusually good eyesight.

Louis Rosenbaum was an ophthalmologist with the Los Angeles Dodgers in the late 80s and early 90s. He became curious when exceptional hitters tested as having exceptional eyesight. So Rosenbaum developed a new vision test that could test vision to 20/8, *the theoretical limits of human eyesight.*[14]

After Rosenbaum developed the new vision test, Tommy Lasorda, the legendary Dodgers manager, challenged him to try to predict which minor league players would thrive in the majors, using only eyesight data.

In his second year of using the new test, Rosenbaum picked a catcher in the minors named Mike Piazza. In 1988, Piazza was drafted in the 62nd round as the 1039th player taken in the draft. However, after Rosenbaum tested his vision and chose him, Mike Piazza went on to win the National League Rookie of the Year in 1993 and became the greatest hitting catcher in baseball history.

So, why is vision so important?

David Epstein, author of *The Sports Gene: The Inside Science to Athletic Performance*, writes:

"Baseball players have to know before the final two hundred milliseconds of a pitch where to swing, so the earlier they pick up anticipatory cues, the better."

Baseball players are making decisions on how to swing the bat **before** the ball has completely left the pitcher's hand, not when it is in the air. By that time, it would be speeding toward them at 90+mph and it would be too late to make a decision.

Great players can see the red seams of a ball spinning in a pattern as the ball leaves the pitcher's hand and can then decide how to swing.

That is mind-blowing! They are reacting to details that no one else can see until we all watch the replay in slow motion.

Rome revamped their city and army. Baseball players make split-second decisions about their reaction to a pitch due to exceptional eyesight that reveals things others cannot see.

What do details offer you?

Rome contrasted their systems of protection against attack with how those systems were destroyed. Did the use of contrast and noticing details work for them? Yes!

They began winning battles and became conquerors, rather than being on the defensive.

About 100 years later, they came into conflict with hill tribes called the Samnites. They fought for almost 50 years, but the Romans continued to learn, adjust, and finally won. Their ability to change their military strategy helped them become a regional power, and their continually renewed military system became the foundation of the new Empire.

By their pinnacle of power, the Romans knew how many soldiers to send to a battle based not only the size of the enemy's army, but also on the details of the surrounding population, size and quality of fields and terrain. They had perfected the art of war and were able to focus on logistics, further crushing their enemies. They found victory in observing and learning from the small details. They used facts to their advantage.

The Romans became champions, and one difference between champions and everyone else is how they handle defeat.

> A champion will look at every minute detail, pick apart the entire scenario, and figure out what changes need to be made to improve (even if they are radical).

The champion doesn't fall prey to making excuses such as: "it was a lucky break" or "we can't change, because we've always done it that way." The champion takes the time to gather details, and then uses them to build clarity and achieve success.

Take time to fill in the details on your Living Visual. Beginning with facts means searching for all facts, no matter how small or seemingly insignificant.

6 *Build Community*

Have you heard someone refer to a situation like being a "canary in a coal mine?" It comes from coal miners in the 1800s carrying canaries with them down into mine shafts. If a buildup of toxic gas happened, the bird would stop singing and die, alerting the miners that it was time to exit the shaft or suffer the same fate.

We need canaries singing in our lives. Not just one, lots of them! We go down into the deep mine shafts of our careers, marriages, parenting, relationships, or education and can some-times hit an unexpected problem.

When we focus on our priorities in creating movement, the very thing that helps us move can create a problem, if left unchecked.

We need people involved in our lives who descend into the shafts with us, just like canaries. It is our responsibility to invite them into those spaces and listen to their feedback. If we decide to go-it-alone, we risk suffering many hardships that will inevitably catch us off guard, just like a gas build-up in the mine. *We need to build community.*

No one lives and operates on an island or achieves lasting success in a vacuum. We need other people and they need us.

Community gives participants several key benefits, as it relates to clarity. Think of community as an enhancer or multiplier. When we share our lives in diverse communities, we enhance or multiply the effects of all the other clarity-cultivating tactics.

Consider these examples of how living in community will help you generate clarity:

1 *Wisdom from diverse experience.*
By living in community, we are often exposed to people who have "been there/done that." The variety of experiences offers us a resource to generate greater clarity, which can speed up building a clear picture, help highlight and uncover confusion, and expand our vision.

2 *Reshape distorted frames.*
Distorted frames can hinder our ability to see a true reality and generate real clarity. By combining and overlaying the diverse frames of the community, it is possible to reshape our frame to one that is more in line with true reality. This diversity enhances the way we see the world.

3 *Enhance Awareness.*
In a community, we can have trusting relationships, be vulnerable, and give others the opportunity to question our

lives or problems. A caring community can be a safe environment where we can find encouragement to exploit gifts that may have otherwise gone overlooked, thus enhancing our self-awareness.

4 *Reinforce Core Values.*
When we face difficult situations or tough decisions, we must make choices that may have moral and ethical consequences. Caring communities can help affirm and reinforce our core values to sustain us making the best choices. If our friends are caring, authentic, and wise, they will help us guard against destructive desires and move on productive core values. Like the philosopher and rapper Ice Cube once said, "You better check yo'self before you wreck yo'self!"

When we need clarity, we need community.

Community is not social media groups. Online communities are loosely bound by sharing common information about similar interests, like pins on Pinterest. This is a bit community-ish, but isn't the kind of community we are discussing here.

Before Facebook and social media, there was an interest I had when I was a kid that also had an association I could join, called the numismatic association. And just what in the world is a numismatic? A coin collector!

When I was young, and apparently super-nerdy, I became fascinated with old coins. I found out that you could become a member of a coin collectors club and be a part of a coin collecting community!

For a membership fee, they sent me a red book with all the current coin values and even threw in a membership card to boot. What a great deal! I was a professional coin collector at eight-years-old. I then talked my parents into taking me to a coin show. Who knew coin shows even existed?

When we got there, I realized a couple of facts. First, collecting coins is an expensive hobby for an 8-year-old. Second, I was not a professional and was no more in a coin collecting community than a random guy walking outside the building.

Building community is how we go about weaving people into the fabric of our lives so we can be honest and open about important issues. It is, therefore, important that we ask ourselves if the people we are building into a community are credible and sincere. Whether they are people who respond with the truth as they see it – or are bobbleheads that just agree with us.

Take time to reflect on the people in your life that are trustworthy, vulnerable, and credible. Have you been honest with them? Use those people to help you gain clarity, but also to become a better you.

Clarity Begets . . . Clarity.

What is one of the best ways to gain a more defined Living Visual? By looking at the clarity you already have about the picture. It may sound crazy, but clarity has a compounding effect.

Think about it, what are the easiest pieces to place when you are putting together a 1000-piece, square or rectangle puzzle? The first four pieces and the last four pieces. No matter how many pieces the puzzle has, anyone can quickly find the four corner pieces, and later, the last four pieces, because the choices are so limited. Your puzzle-piece-placing-speed accelerates as you near the finish, because it becomes more and more obvious where to place each piece.

Putting a puzzle together requires moving from the general to the specific. The general includes what picture the puzzle creates and the specific includes the shape of the pieces and the relationship between the pieces. We focus on the details by investigating how each individual piece connects to the surrounding pieces and how it fits into the view of the whole.

As we move, we build a picture with more and more clarity. Every time we take one step forward, by putting one piece in place, it makes it possible to place the next piece.

We also become more confident in our puzzle-piece-placing the further down the road of clarity we travel.

The last four pieces are easy to place, because we have eliminated all other options. We are so focused on such a small area and so few pieces; it's like we don't really have a choice. We are committed to placing those four pieces only in those four empty spots.

When we are trying to close gaps in our lives or our businesses, building clarity is just like putting together a puzzle. The more we fit in place, the easier it becomes to see the next move. A technical term used in project management to capture this phenomenon is *progressive elaboration*.

In large IT projects, the developers may not be able to determine all the problems and challenges they will face throughout the entire project, so they focus on short-term goals and building a good foundation, and then look at the whole project in pieces. Get one in place, and then look at the work that is left.

If you are graduating high school or college and feel pressure to know exactly what your career is going to be – relax! Life is much messier, colorful, confusing, frustrating, and beautiful than your syllabus. You may set out to be a microbiologist and be in the same field for 40 years. However, you may *think* you are going to be a microbiologist, and after graduation not be able to find a job. And twenty years from graduation, you will look back in amazement at the journey life has taken you.

If we are in a period of transition, we seek clarity. Sometimes that means placing one piece, one step before the next. Each step is movement. Each step lightens and focuses the next. Clarity begets clarity.

Chapter 4

Powerful Clarity

I am seeking, I am striving, I am in it with all of my heart.

– Vincent van Gogh

We have defined clarity as three major parts: light, focus, and frame.

We discussed cultivating clarity to produce *meaningful* action by implementing seven tactics: Uncover Confusion, Begin with Facts, Build Community, Leverage Experience, Develop Awareness, Trust Core Values, and Leverage Existing Clarity.

Now, with the basics of clarity in mind, let's discuss the strategy for maximizing clarity in our lives.

Our goal is to produce powerful clarity. And what is that, exactly? And why is it important?

It is more than seeing the available options. It is creating a picture in your mind that is so vivid and compelling that you can't help but want to create it.

Powerful clarity is like the dream you had one night that you were disappointed wasn't real when you woke up the next morning. It is so strong that once you have the picture in your head – it is impossible to forget.

> Powerful clarity begins with an *end in mind*[15] so compelling that it produces deep emotional energy that drives us to make it reality.

Can we build clarity that actually gives us the energy to create movement? Yes!

The image you create must be powerful enough to entice your commitment. It must be something that you not only **should** do, but something you <u>want</u> to do.

When we see something so amazing, so captivating, and so compelling, we will move toward it with relentless perseverance.

Can you produce a picture of where you want to be that is so clear and compelling that you feel deep emotion when you think about it?

We gladly exert great energy in activities that will produce the picture we have created. The greater the clarity and focus of our activities, the greater likelihood we will produce the picture we have constructed in our mind.

And when our picture is compelling and clear, something happens . . . **we start believing it is possible!**

You may have a great map to guide you from New York to California, but if you don't *believe* you can make the journey, you will never start the trip.

Belief is energizing. The bigger the barrier or obstacle, the harder the task, the more impossible the mission – the more important it is to believe we can do it. We may or may not make it, but we are 100% guaranteed to fail if we don't believe.

When our clarity creates deep emotion and belief, our confidence grows. It's a waterfall effect that cascades through our life. We ride that confidence, maximize our clarity, and power our movement forward. BOOM!

Now you know the value and power of emotion and belief in

maximizing the power of your clarity. However, there are certain things that reduce the power of our clarity.

What limits our ability to see clearly or produce powerful clarity?

Mindful Quadrant

When I was a kid we still used radios with dials and rabbit-ear antennas on our TV. I remember having to stand at the TV and hold the antenna in the perfect position or the show wouldn't come in clearly. Too far to the right or left and all we saw was static. Too much or too little? Too far or too close? That was me questioning my brothers before watching our favorite show.

If we want to build powerful clarity, we have to start balancing our antennas to make sure we produce the clearest picture.

This is called being mindful – keenly aware and thoughtful about our present state.

The Mindful Quadrants helps us to create powerful clarity.

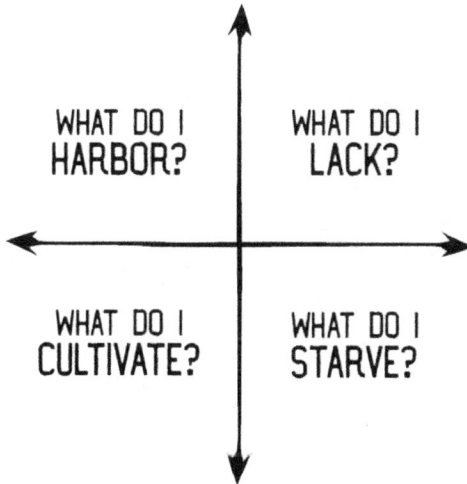

WHAT DO I
HARBOR?

WHAT DO I
LACK?

WHAT DO I
CULTIVATE?

WHAT DO I
STARVE?

fig. 3a
THE MINDFUL QUADRANT

These four questions help you balance your *antennas* to make sure you are producing the maximum clarity signal.

The list below sums up the purpose of each question.

Harbor – When you harbor something, you protect it and keep it safe. You shield it from the outside, so it remains undisturbed.

Lack – This represents a deficiency. You need it, but do not have enough of it. We are missing something that would make us whole. This question exposes areas of our lives we can improve by practicing, acquiring, or learning something new.

Cultivate – When we cultivate something, we put energy and organization to it so it will grow. We feed it, water it, weed around it, and nurture it, because it produces something we deem valuable.

Starve – When we starve something, we suppress, limit, and neglect it. We intentionally work against giving it the resources it needs to thrive.

It can be easy to answer these four questions too quickly and without enough consideration. So, before you give your answers, flip back to the sections on Develop Awareness and Build Community. Then, take time to meditate, reflect, and pray.

Another beneficial step would be to take someone to lunch and invite them to answer the four questions (about you).

You can also offer this invitation to coaches, counselors, leaders or pastors, as their answers can help us work through the questions from alternative viewpoints. Every new bit of information adds to the data you're gathering toward producing clarity.

Once we answer these four questions, we can see how our Mindful Quadrants are working.

If our Mindful Quadrants balance looks like the one below, we will be unable to produce powerful clarity.

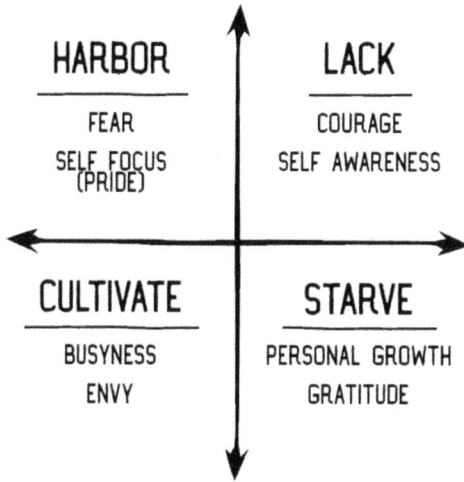

```
              HARBOR    |    LACK
              ──────    |    ────
               FEAR     |   COURAGE
            SELF FOCUS   | SELF AWARENESS
              (PRIDE)    |
          ───────────────┼───────────────→
             CULTIVATE   |    STARVE
             ─────────   |    ──────
              BUSYNESS   | PERSONAL GROWTH
               ENVY      |    GRATITUDE
```

fig. 3b
UNBALANCED QUADRANTS

Why would the chart above limit or distort our clarity?

The four Quadrants are out of balance and reveal that we are protecting things we should be lacking or starving, and starving things we should be cultivating.

Take the top left quadrat. When we harbor fear, we don't just experience fear, we protect the fear. We protect our right to be afraid and live in fear. Fear distorts our frames and keeps us from seeing potential opportunities and reality, so we lose the ability to build accurate and powerful clarity.

And then, the top right quadrant. We lack or are missing something that would make us whole. If we lack self-awareness, we miss an opportunity to paint a picture of what we really want.

We may feel pressure to paint a mental picture that someone else wants for us or one that doesn't line up with our strengths and skills. If we are living out someone else's dream for our life, our clarity will never be powerful or capture our imagination. We will lack the energy necessary to drive movement.

Then, bottom left quadrant. This is what we expend energy on building. What happens when we cultivate other more negative attributes, like busyness? When we are busy, we have less time to reflect and work on cultivating clarity or creating real meaningful movement. *We create a lot of motion, but not a lot of movement.* When we get to the end of a busy day and do not feel like we have accomplished anything, we are cultivating the wrong activities.

And finally, the bottom right quadrant. This is what we starve, things that we want to wither or waste away. We don't feed them. They shrink and slowly disappear. What happens when we starve positive things, like personal growth? We don't grow.

Lack of personal growth is a sure-fire way to ensure you become stuck in a rut.

When we stop pushing and challenging ourselves and stop renewing our minds, our spirit begins to slowly wither. When we wither, we lose the desire to create clarity in the first place. We don't close the gaps in our lives. We act as though they don't exist.

How would you answer the Mindful Quadrants questions? Are there answers you listed that will keep you from creating powerful clarity?

It is important to be aware of how, where, and when the answers to the Mindful Quadrants questions are active in your life. This is not an easy exercise.

The reason I named it Mindful Quadrants is because it requires us to honestly take stock of our lives in ways that may be uncomfortable or even painful. It requires us to look honestly at ourselves to see where internal gaps may be limiting movement.

It requires mindfulness.

Below is one example of quadrants for someone who could build powerful clarity.

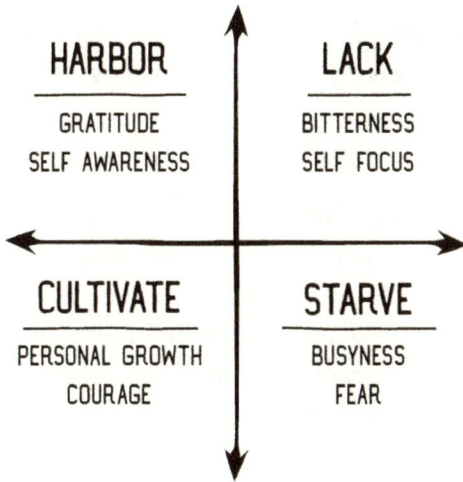

```
        HARBOR    |    LACK
        ───────   |    ────
       GRATITUDE  |  BITTERNESS
     SELF AWARENESS|  SELF FOCUS
   ←──────────────┼──────────────→
       CULTIVATE  |    STARVE
       ─────────  |    ──────
   PERSONAL GROWTH|   BUSYNESS
       COURAGE    |     FEAR
```

fig. 3c
BALANCED QUADRANTS

Pillar I Review

You now have an understanding of the language of clarity and how to build powerful clarity in your life.

From the clarity building blocks to the seven tactics used to cultivate clarity to the power of emotion and belief to maximize the power of your clarity, you now know how to drive your movement toward who you want to be and where you want to go.

One last warning: Don't use perfect clarity as an excuse for lack of movement.

If we must know *everything in full detail* before we are willing to move, it probably means we are struggling with balancing at least one of the Mindful Quadrants.

Remember, we want to develop powerful clarity in our mind to help us make decisions, motivate us, and give us direction. We must be careful to not use the lack of details in our picture to keep us from moving at all.

> *There is always tension between waiting to develop too much clarity and moving before knowing enough details.*

The goal of seeking clarity is not to seek until we know every-thing. The goal is to seek until **we know enough to move**.

Clarity should help us move from the general to the specific, continually re-focusing and sharpening our picture.

Yet with all the distractions, emotions, and noise in our lives, how do we find the time to produce that picture?

We learn how to set boundaries . . .

Wait . . . not ready to finish working on clarity? No problem! Please visit www.ThinkMoveThrive.com/resources to download a list of questions and other resources and tools you can use at work, home, or school to help you generate more clarity in your life.

Pillar II
Develop Boundaries

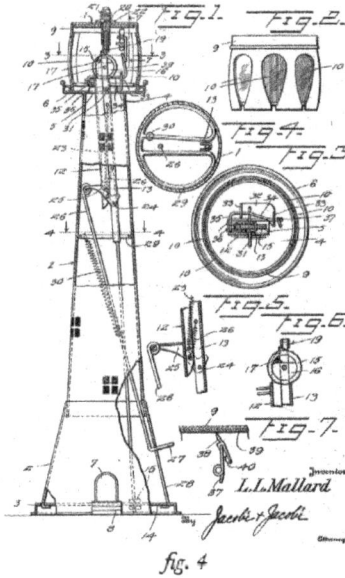

fig. 4

A man without self-control is like a city broken into and left without walls.

– Proverbs 25:28

We are finite creatures. However, it is amazing how often we forget that simple fact. We take our kids to every soccer practice, music lesson, tutor session, and every dance recital with some hope that they are going to master six foreign languages, be the captain of the soccer team, and someday run for public office, after coming off their world music tour.

We over-book, double book, and take time management courses to squeeze 36 hours of activities into 24 hours each day. We need our news faster, our coffee stronger, and our waistlines thinner than ever before, and we plan on achieving our goals by simply sleeping less and getting more done.

Eventually, our finite inner-self says: "Hold on!"

And we have to face that we've made the mistake of assuming that "activity is synonymous with achievement" as the great coach, John Wooden, said.

Life is full of choices or tradeoffs that determine our experiences, and our experiences form who we become.

So, when we hear the word boundaries, we may associate it with being restricted, a negative obstacle. Like, all the things your parents said you couldn't do. All the places you couldn't go. All the rules your school or company asks you to follow.

We may feel like boundaries limit our choices and, therefore, limit our experience and happiness. However, setting boundaries in our lives and our businesses has the opposite effect.

When we set proper boundaries we actually have deeper, more meaningful experiences that produce more happiness and a greater return on our efforts. It is a paradox: less is more.

Boundaries help us make fewer, more meaningful, choices which increase the likelihood that the future or outcome we create is in line with our Living Visual.

Every time we make a choice, we make a tradeoff. Every time we make a choice, we have a chance of missing something in the trade. By limiting our choices, we save time and make it easier to navigate through the tradeoffs of available options. By evaluating fewer tradeoffs, we tend to make better choices.

Think about the picture of the lighthouse. It represents a boundary between the land and the sea.

Before seeing the lighthouse signal, a ship captain has four choices: forward, backward, left, or right (assuming he doesn't drop achor). After seeing the signal, he has three choices: backward, left, or right.

The lighthouse limits his choices, but not his freedom of movement. On the contrary, the ship is free to continue sailing when it heeds the distant signal of approaching land.

It is also important to note that boundaries can be abused and misused.

Boundaries draw lines of distinction and keep us safe, like in the example of the lighthouse. However, sometimes we can misuse boundaries and try to use them to control *everything* in our lives.

If we build boundaries to keep the world out or think that we can eliminate all chaos or tragedy in our lives, we can create an unhealthy mental state.

If we approach boundaries from a fear of the unknown, we can set boundaries that are so limiting we can't achieve our goals.

The lighthouse protects those who sail their ships up the coast. The lighthouse is irrelevant to those who fear getting on a boat. As we Develop Boundaries, it is important to be aware of the motives behind our boundaries.

In this part, we will unpack the role of boundaries, setting proper boundaries, and the differences between barriers and boundaries.

Chapter 5

The Role of Boundaries

No man is free who is not a master of himself.

– Epictetus

Boundaries measure how serious we are about moving, how much clarity we have cultivated, and how intense our response is toward achieving the mental picture we have created.

When we gain true clarity about exactly what we want, it increases our motivation to achieve it.

Boundaries intentionally limit certain actions and energy to focus our limited resources on accomplishing what is most important in our lives.

Boundaries are less about the willpower to do or not to do certain things and more about identity. They are lines that *define* and set apart something unique. We build boundaries in our lives to create or reinforce something new and unique.

When we create a mental picture so clear it compels us to move, boundaries ensure that our movement is limited to activities that are in line with that mental picture.

I love the proverb: "A man without self-control is like a city broken into and left without walls." It offers us such a vivid visual picture of what a person is like with no self-control, no boundaries.

Think of an ancient walled city. Thousands of man hours were spent erecting these great walls, which were the only way the city could control what and who was allowed into or out of the city. The walls became boundaries, part of the city's culture and permanent structure.

Yet no one inside the ancient city would have said, "Look at these walls, they are so restrictive. I wish we could knock them down so I wouldn't have to walk all the way to the front gate to go out in the countryside." They knew and understood that any inconvenience caused by the wall was in their best interest.

The wall helped them sleep at night, knowing that a band of marauders could not ride into their city and burn their houses down. The wall helped them protect themselves, their families, and their resources; and allowed them to work without fear of attack.

The walls gave freedom to the people inside the city.

Just like how the ancient cultures built city walls, we need to intentionally build walls – boundaries – to maximize movement in our work and life.

In business, boundaries may define employee roles and responsibilities to help them focus on what is most important to the team.

Boundaries may also mean trashing all the products or services that do not add true value to the customer, and instead, focusing on what deliverables the company can be *best in class* at providing.

Remember how LEGO ran into trouble when they blurred the lines and began operating outside the "walls" they had built around their blocks?

At home, boundaries may mean setting a time our kids must turn off all electronic devices or go to bed, so the family can interact and everyone can get enough sleep for school the next day. Boundaries might mean that you don't watch TV until after you and your spouse have communicated, one-on-one, for thirty minutes about the day.

These examples may sound trivial or of little value. They may also seem like things that just rule or limit certain behaviors.

> *If we only see the boundary or wall, we will only see them as restrictions.*

Boundaries have to emerge from clarity. If we see a clear picture of our family building deep and meaningful connections, learning and growing together, then turning off electronic devices is not restrictive at all. In fact, turning off the devices gives the family free time to build their relationships.

When we struggle to achieve our goals, many times it is because we either lack proper boundaries or our boundaries are not clearly defined or our boundaries are out of alignment with our Living Visual.

If you are exhausted and super busy, but feel like you never accomplish anything, <u>you have a boundary problem</u>.

Without a compelling Living Visual, we lack the guidance needed to make critical decisions on how to spend our time and resources. That is why boundaries tend to follow or emerge from clarity. If we struggle setting boundaries, we need more clarity.

It makes no sense to re-organize the company or turn off our kid's electronic devices without answering the compelling question: "why?"

The following pages will unpack the benefits and role of boundaries in our lives. There are six benefits we produce when we set proper boundaries:

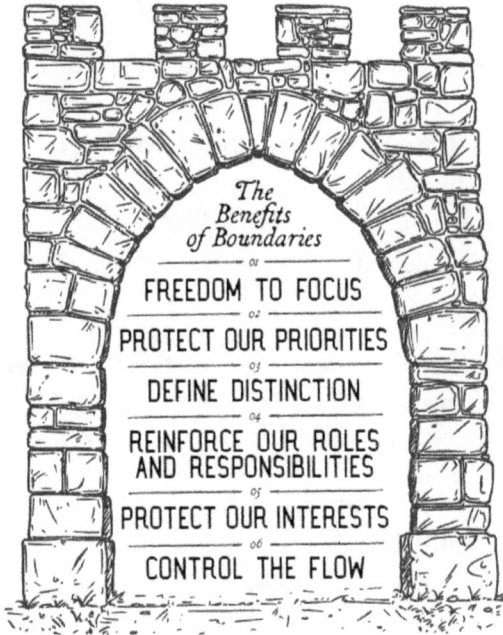

fig. 5
THE BENEFITS OF BOUNDARIES

1 – Freedom to Focus

George Lucas, the creator of Star Wars, said: "Always remember: your focus determines your reality." How true.

If we are not living in the reality that makes us happy, we need to take the time to think about our focus or lack of focus.

When we take stock of our lives, we desperately want to know that our efforts matter or have meaning. We want to be loved and to love, to know and be known. It is tempting, in a world full of social media, to become too focused *on someone we think we want to be like,* instead of *who we are today.*

We must ground our focus on things that are important today in our own lives. Our focus should rest on the activities needed to produce the type of person we want to become. If we catch ourselves focusing on other people, their lives, their kids, their jobs, their happiness, it is important to step back and focus on the life we are creating for ourselves.

So many times, shiny things distract us. Instead of comparing ourselves to others; we can ask ourselves the question: "Are you being the best *you* for others?"

We may be in a difficult season of life, everyone has them, but even in difficult situations we still can choose how and where we direct our focus.

> *We can focus on the difficulties – or we can choose to focus on the tasks we need to accomplish to move past or through the obstacle.*

Focusing on our difficulties produces negative emotions, self-pity, and stagnation. Don't feel sorry, feel better. Focusing on the solution produces energy, hope, and encouragement as you see the results of your response. The hope: do more, while doing less.

Consider this: Have you ever gone on vacation and left your phone at home? Maybe it wasn't a vacation, but just a trip to the drug store. You stepped out of your car, reached for your phone and, oh no – it's gone! Panic sets in. But after you remember that your phone is at home on the kitchen counter, the reality sets in.

You are free.

Free from distractions, calls, social media posts, emails from work and all the other things that the phone can "help" you do every day.

It is now possible for you to completely focus on where you are in the present moment.

The moment we leave our phone on the counter, we start focusing more on the present moment. We may drive better (no texts or phone calls), notice more details in our surroundings, and speak to more people at the store, simply because we aren't distracted. **Having to choose** between our phone and other activities of the present **is removed**.

Boundaries help us direct our focus in the present moment. The horizon of tomorrow is always in our peripheral vision, but our eyes are focused on the task at hand.

When we are serious about moving toward a goal or Living Visual, we will *intentionally* block out all those distractions and things of lesser value.

Developing boundaries clears the table of every distraction that keeps us from focusing on what is most important.

If we want to move, we need the freedom to focus.

2 – Protect our Priorities

We protect our priorities to limit distractions and apply maximum effort towards accomplishing what matters most to us. Developing Boundaries helps prioritize the activities or areas of our life that require the most attention for us to be happy.

Have you ever been busy all day, and then, at the end of the day, felt remorse when you asked yourself: "What did I do today?"

> **We feel remorse when we spend too much time on things we care too little about.**

Every day we are threatened with dozens of distractions that can burn energy and time, but accomplish nothing. Consider the co-workers who love to involve you in mindless chatting. Then, there are the times you take on tasks that have little or nothing to do with your duties at work. The 'ping' of a new email. Not to mention, demanding phone calls or face-to-face meetings requiring your time and energy.

And don't forget the allure of social media. It's possible to log on to Facebook, Instagram, SnapChat, or any other social media app and trade valuable time for less meaningful activity. For many of us, this one time-trap supersedes all others. Busy, yet empty.

Energy with no direction is like a Top Fuel dragster warming up for a race. These are the fastest-accelerating race cars in the world, and before they approach the start line, they heat and clean their tires by performing a burnout. Tires are spinning and the engine is screaming. Smoke billows out so thick no one can see the wheels, and yet there is no forward movement!

Where does 10,000 horsepower go when it is not applied in a direction? *Up in smoke.*

When we prioritize what matters most and have the Freedom to Focus on the present, it releases our stored potential. We are able to use our energy on work that is important to us. We become a Top Fuel dragster running wide open down the track. And when we finish our day's work, we feel satisfied, because we worked on something we believe is worthy of our energy. Our priorities are worth protecting and building walls around.

Boundaries are the protection we construct to fend off the dangerous enemy named, *Worthless Activity.* When we eliminate the need to choose between social media and work, emails and family time, or working out and television, we create intentional, meaningful movement towards important things that matter to us.

Can you identify your priorities, the things that are necessary to maintain the quality of life you need to create movement and be happy?

Can you imagine fortifying these things, making them so special, of such high priority, that you can easily focus on them and not be distracted by lesser-order things?

What steps can you take right now to protect your priorities and simplify or remove unnecessary distractions?

3 – Embrace Natural Boundaries

Boundaries are as much about defining what you are, as what you are not.

I was always fascinated in biology when the class could look under the microscope. The unseen world of cells and bacteria was intriguing. One point that stood out to me was the distinction between plant and animal cells. Many times, the plant cells were rigid and enclosed by a strong wall of cellulose. They looked like building blocks, all stacked on top of each other, and could not change their shape.

Animal cells, on the contrary, were rounded or oval-shaped, with only a thin membrane. The cells were much less rigid and could even change shape. The walls of the cells defined what type of cell it was and even its characteristics.

The walls that we construct in our lives define who we are at a fundamental level, because they determine our focus. Our focus determines our choices, and our choices determine our future selves.

Plant and animal cells have cell walls that they did not choose. They are natural boundaries. We all have natural boundaries, too.

For example, I am not seven feet tall and I have a low vertical leap. The likelihood that I will ever dunk a basketball is extremely low. This is not a problem, just a definition.

Natural boundaries help us make decisions. Am I better at math or language? Am I coordinated or a little clumsy? Do I excel in music or dance?

> *Rather than bemoan the natural boundaries we have been given, we should embrace them.*

Remember the millions of decisions you make each day? Knowing your natural boundaries helps you make more accurate and quicker decisions. This awareness will also keep you from making decisions that would waste your time and focus.

Defining your natural boundaries allows us to make decisions based on who we are and who we are striving to be, and when you focus on being yourself, that focus gives you the ability to be your BEST self.

4 – Reinforce Responsibility and Accountability

"You go out there and tell those jackasses to rip all those pipes out and start over. Tell them they are going to do it right or else!"

This was my boss shouting out instructions to me – the newbie college grad project engineer – on my first real project, the construction of a dormitory. Being ordered to boss men with one hundred times my experience around on the job site made me as nervous as a cat in tin foil shoes.

My boss, Joe, was listed as the construction manager on this job. We were performing oversight during the project for the owner. This meant we inspected the project during construction and pointed out any mistakes the general contractor and sub-contractors made, so the project was done right. So, it's easy to see why the general contractor wasn't excited to have us on site.

Joe was an older gentleman, who had recently been laid off from a large engineering firm in town. He was just a year or two from retirement when this happened. And now, he was stuck in a dirty job site trailer, with a green, twenty-something, surrounded by construction workers who considered him an outsider and his reason for being there irritating at the least, a threat at the worst.

It was miserable.

His one happy place was reading the paper each day and believe me, he read every line.

On this particular day, he had learned that the plumbers on the 3rd floor had installed the piping incorrectly and planned on letting the sheetrock crew cover it up without correcting it.

That was when he put down his paper, looked at me and said, "You go out there and tell those . . ."

I sat on my broken, dirty chair in the corner of the tiny job site trailer office and thought about the consequences of carrying out his orders.

These were men who had been builders before I was born. If I confronted their mistake, they might show me some technical detail, beyond my experience or expertise, and argue that they had no choice but to construct the pipes in that fashion. How could I contest their explanations? I had been onsite for only a month.

None of the scenarios I envisioned ended with the client receiving quality construction.

So, I took some risk when I said, "Joe, I can't do that. I will be happy to go with you and you can show me what the problem is, why it is a problem, and how we want to correct it. But I can't go up there by myself, because we both know the result will not be good."

Joe sat back and stared at me. I waited to see if he would tell me to do it anyway, which would mean he would be avoiding his responsibility. Oversight rested on his shoulders, as construction manager.

He finally gave me a nod, put down his paper, and said, "Come on, let's go."

Joe did what many of us do almost every day: he tried to delegate his accountability. Boundaries don't allow that.

> ✴ *As a leader, you can delegate a role, but you cannot delegate accountability.*

Joe was held accountable for the work being done correctly. He had credibility with all the workers. He had been on the job site since day one. He had seen the dormitory rise out of the dirt and had been meeting with the contractors, architects, and engineers on a regular basis. He was the right man to make the call on the piping and communicate that a change was required.

But . . . he was in his happy place, reading the paper. It was cold outside and warm in our trailer. He knew the guys would be angry and he would face some resistance. So, he shucked his responsibility and tried to hand it to me.

Movement is rejecting complacency. Movement is accepting responsibility <u>and</u> being accountable for the results. Boundaries help us define our responsibilities and roles.

Let's consider responsibility and accountability.

A responsibility would be some activity that is related to a person's strengths or role. Say your spouse is good with numbers. This might mean that your spouse assumes the responsibility of creating and managing the family's finances.

Accountability would be an obligation specifically assigned to you. For example, if only your name is on your house mortgage, the bank won't care who manages the budget, because the accountability lies with the name of the person who inked the contract.

Responsibilities are activities we perform to help us and those around us to accomplish goals. Accountability is being held liable for producing certain results.

My roles on the construction site were safety inspector and project engineer. These roles loosely defined my duties, which were to conduct safety inspections several times a day, fill out paperwork, relay messages to our corporate office, and learn the art and science of managing a construction project.

I was held accountable to make sure all work areas conformed to safe work environment standards, so there were no job site injuries.

Joe's role was site construction manager. His responsibilities covered upper-management meetings with the owners, architects, and engineers, reviewing change orders, and giving status updates to the owner.

He was accountable to make sure the work that was completed adhered to the specifications and maintained high quality.

What are your responsibilities and for what are you accountable? Do you remain true to them or do you push them off on others, then push any blame for poor results onto someone else?

To start moving, it's best to own your responsibilities, guard them, focus on them, and hold yourself accountable to move toward your goal.

5 – Protect Our Interests

The most obvious relation of the opening Proverb, and our lives, is protection.

What is the role of walls in ancient cities? To protect the people inside them.

Many times, the boundaries in our lives are put in place to keep us out of physical, mental and emotional danger. Parents on the playground shout at sons and daughters to not go backward up the slide, thus setting boundaries for the safety of their kids.

Like having the Disney character, Jiminy Cricket, sit on our shoulder reminding us that "just because you can, doesn't mean you should," boundaries help us make sure the activities we engage in will not be destructive.

If we miss setting up the proper boundaries in our life or business, we put ourselves at risk.

Complacency, fear, apathy and ignorance are tremendous enemies of boundaries.

On May 4, 1988, about 10 miles southeast of Las Vegas, the residents of Clark County, NV experienced the largest domestic, non-nuclear explosion in recorded history.[16]

The Pacific Engineering Production Company of Nevada (PEPCON) was producing a chemical, Ammonium Perchlorate (AP), which is a major component used by NASA in rocket fuel.

Almost 70% (382 tons by weight) of the Space Shuttle Solid Rocket Booster is AP, which launches the shuttle into space.

AP is extremely dangerous; and when mixed with *aluminum and certain plastics,* creates the type of explosion that can power a rocket.

The initial problems did not start on that windy day in May. Arguably, they began in Cape Canaveral, almost two years earlier, in January 1986 when the Challenger Space Shuttle exploded on live television. The response by the US Government was to ground NASA's space program for two years. President Ronald Regan established the Rogers Commission to investigate the accident.

The Rogers Commission gave the following report excerpts to the President: *"Complacency, and failures in supervision and reporting, seriously aggravated these risks."*

The warnings given by the Rogers commission focused on building proper organizational boundaries within NASA to reduce the likelihood of catastrophe.

So, what does the Challenger disaster have to do with PEPCON?

The grounded space program meant NASA no longer needed shuttle rocket fuel. PEPCON should have dramatically cut back the production of AP to match the lower demand. However, they had a government contract to produce a specified amount of AP. So, they kept churning it out. Realizing their over-production, they decided to store the excess AP in *polyethylene drums* and *aluminum bins.*

Before the explosion, they had accrued over 10,000 plastic drums of AP, each weighing 550 pounds, not realizing that plastics and aluminum were the additives that maximize the power of AP.[17]

PEPCON had successfully made AP for US government contracts since the 1950s without any major incident. They had experienced small fires in the plant and had contained them with nothing more than a garden hose.

For more than 30 years, they had a track record of success. That success led to complacency.

Complacency translated into not realizing all the AP dust accumulating all over the flat surfaces of the plant. Complacency meant that no sprinkler or alarm system was installed in the plant.

Amazingly, the engineers, managers, workers, and safety inspectors at the plant were aware of the dangers of AP and its potential power. The entire plant was knowingly operating out of compliance with the US National Fire Protection Association (NFPA) code 43 (1980). The plant was required to have automatic fire detection, deluge sprinkler protection, an emergency plan, and periodic training exercises conducted with local first responders.

Complacency does not care about codes; and therefore, none of these measures were put into place.

So, at 11:30 am May 4th, two employees were repairing the plant's steel and fiberglass drying structure. Sparks from their welding torch ignited some of the fiberglass building material. The workers tried to fight the fire with a garden hose. By 11:51, the fire response teams were contacted. By 11:53, multiple 55-gallon drums exploded into a fireball.

Luckily, supervisor radios had worked to inform the workers to evacuate the premises immediately (as if the giant fireball didn't).

By 11:57, the fire had reached the storage area where a majority of the AP was in plastic drums.

In one explosion, 1500 tons were consumed. Remember, a space shuttle rocket booster contains about 382 tons. So, in that one explosion, registering 3.5 on the Richter scale, almost four times the amount consumed by the shuttle booster flying into space was ignited.

In the aftermath of the explosion 372 people were injured, two were killed, and the explosion inflicted over 70 million dollars of damage to structures in a 10-mile radius. While it is amazing that only two people lost their lives in the catastrophe, the event never should have happened.

Ironically in 2012 NASA reviewed the PEPCON accident and produced a case study on how it happened and could have been prevented. The same people chastised by the Rogers Commission made this statement about PEPCON:

"Planning for failure, like designing for success, sometimes depends upon key assumptions to scope and scale the effort to the resources available."

Boundaries help us plan for failure and design for success. NASA learned after Challenger and saw the problems with leaning on complacency.

What boundaries do you have in place in your life to keep you safe? What boundaries have you established that prevent you from becoming complacent?

6 – Control the Flow

I was on another flight to the west coast. I was out of breath and a bit perturbed because my layover had been delayed and I had to hustle through the airport to catch my flight. However, the flight got delayed on the tarmac. A gentleman in the seat beside me leaned over and made a joke about how I had been late only to be delayed again. We started talking about work and families, and it ended up being one of the most fascinating conversations of all my plane travels.

He was a cereal scientist. Well, not exactly. He worked for a chemical company that serves the food industry and told me the story of vitamins and cereal.

Have you ever wondered how a breakfast cereal can say it has 100% of your daily recommended vitamins, in a single serving? Just how does a cereal maker get all those nutrients packed into your cornflakes?

They bake them into the ingredients, right? Nope, vitamins are bitter, so you would taste bitterness when you ate the cereal.

The trick has to do with understanding boundaries.

The cereal companies, with the help of people like the guy sitting next to me, figured out how to get the nutrients past your mouth, without touching your tongue.

They set up a process that goes like this: when cornflakes are dried, a coating of micro-drops of oil is applied. These micro- drops of oil are combined with vitamins in a proprietary method, encapsulating the vitamins inside the micro-drops. These tiny oil droplets do not break down in your mouth, so you can chew the cornflakes, mix them with milk, and never taste the vitamins safely tucked away inside the oil droplets. Once you swallow, the temperature rises, the acidity in your stomach increases, and the oil droplets immediately break down, releasing the vitamins into your body.

The difference in how you experience eating zinc for breakfast is boundaries. Eating zinc sprinkled on your cereal would make you pucker up! But, eating zinc bound inside oil is not even noticeable.

Think of the ancient city walls. The number of traders, foreigners, people from the countryside, and soldiers allowed into the city were all controlled by the city walls and regulated to maximize the benefit of those who lived inside.

Just like the oil that makes the vitamins able to pass through our mouths to add value in our stomachs, the ancient walls controlled the flow of visitors to allow the ones inside to add value to the markets, stables, squares, and livelihood of the city.

When we build proper boundaries around our lives, we create space. Space to breathe and have fun. Space to reflect and sleep. Space that becomes a buffer between us and all the activities outside the boundaries we set. When we lose that buffering space, we tend to become overwhelmed, stressed, depressed, and anxious.

> *Setting boundaries controls the flow of our activities and the open spaces in our lives.*

We need space at home, so we can be ready for work. We need space to make the best choices, like eating healthy to maximize our efforts at the gym.

We live integrated lives . . . *Boundaries circle our whole life.* When we control the flow of activities in our lives by using boundaries that give us space to consider the most effective ways to integrate those activities, we stop filling up our lives with busy "stuff" that may be a waste of time. By controlling the flow of our lives with boundaries that allow the vitamins in, without their bad taste, we will be able to do a few things well, instead of frantically trying to do everything – meaningless and meaningful. Why not live an integrated life filled with fewer activities that bring us true satisfaction?

Do less, accomplish more.

Chapter 6

Setting Proper Boundaries

We must learn our limits. We are all something, but none of us are everything.

– Blaise Pascal

―――――――――――――

Setting boundaries is a measure of your desire to move toward your Living Visual.

If we want to know how badly someone wants something, look at the boundaries they have set up in their life.

For example, are they trying to **finish** the Boston Marathon or **win** the Boston Marathon?

There is a big difference.

For one thing, the level of commitment is dramatically different. The ones who want to win are relentless about controlling their diet and time spent running.

For example, a study of 27,000 runners conducted by Runners World, found that "62 percent of runners who averaged 31-38 miles per week ran a four-hour marathon, or faster. By contrast, only 8.5 percent of those who logged less than six miles per week were done by the four-hour mark."[18]

In one online blog, an elite runner described a 90-mile training regimen she completed in one week. It is easy to see that the level of sacrifice (hours pounding pavement) is directly correlated to the end result (finish time).

Amateur runners try to schedule running around their daily activities. Elite runners schedule their daily activities around their running.

People often say: "I wish I had time to be a . . . go to . . . become a . . ." but what they are really saying is: I do not prioritize that wish over the activities I am currently involved in.

We condition our lack of focus by not setting clear boundaries that flow from clarity about who we are and where we want to be. The resulting lack of boundaries keeps us from achieving our potential, which can produce reoccurring regret.

Boundaries can be unsettling.

Why is that?

Boundaries require us to make decisions – and making decisions can be difficult. If we choose this, we must give up that. If we walk down the left path, we forfeit the opportunity to walk down the right path.

The big question – when prioritizing our activities – is always:

Do I value _____ more than what I am trying to produce in my Living Visual?

> ✴ **Remember, when we say NO to something, we say YES to something else.**

Is your spouse complaining that you work too much? Are they right?

We all know that relationships need time to cultivate and nurture. No time, no relationship. So, if you agree that your spouse is right, then you also agree that you may be valuing time with your work more than you value time with your spouse.

That may sound harsh, but it is easy to expose our true priorities in life when we evaluate how we spend our time and money.

Our actions, every day, reside within the boundaries we set. It is not what we say – it is what we **do** that matters.

So, if we want to change our priority and spend more time with our spouse, we could set the some or all of the following boundaries:

1. Schedule a date with our partner at least every three weeks without kids or other couples.
2. Put down our phones and turn off the TV at 9 pm every night and catch up on the day's activities.
3. Play a game together, board, card, video or sport, such as softball, tag, basketball, fox-n-geese twice a week.
4. Leave work no later than 5:30 pm (if applicable).
5. Reserve one weekend a month to do a project (garden, clean out basement/garage, check bikes for summer use) at our home we can work on together.
6. Pre-schedule all events on my calendar to avoid double-booking open time.

We feel uncomfortable consciously setting boundaries because they force us to choose. We start by doubting ourselves and our decisions. We question our Living Visual and worry about what will happen if we set up poor or incomplete boundaries.

What if we get it wrong?

When my daughters were babies, they all had teething blankets. They even named them, calling them "dackins." As our little girls matured, they became less attached to their dackins. They became a hindrance, instead of a comfort. At some point in their early childhood, they had to make a choice: Do I keep my dackin and miss out on those other activities or give it up? That's a tough choice for a 3-year-old.

We all have our dackins: habits, activities, relationships, and associations that we are a part of, that may have been good at some point in the past but are now limiting our path forward.

What dackin-thing are you holding onto that if given up would make life better?

Setting a boundary means taking control of what we can control.

113

A couple visiting our house one night confessed that they were stressed. They told us how their church was asking them to take on lots of different roles or jobs, in addition to attending services. They would have a job at the service on Sunday morning, and then have another job working with teens during the week. Others had asked them to help in the kid's department.

On top of this, they had a new baby and were exhausted.

The husband said, "We just feel bad saying no because everything they ask us to do needs to be done and is helping others. We have the ability to do it, and it is flattering they would even ask us to help."

Houston, we have a problem. A boundary problem. Do you see how it is possible to get boundaries wrong in our lives and how it can have a dramatic effect on our well-being?

Am I asserting that serving in a church or a community organization is bad? Nope.

Am I asserting that there should never be times in our life when we have a lot on our plate and feel tired? Nope.

> *If we set up the right boundaries in our lives, there may be times we become tired, but instead of feeling burned out, we will feel a sense of accomplishment and pride.*

There may be times your body is tired, but your spirit is full. Just ask any parent of a newborn baby.

If we learn how to set boundaries in our life and work, we will find more meaning in what we do.

To help **Set Proper Boundaries** in our lives, we can use the following three simple steps:

1. **Defining Activities**
2. **Limiting Activities**
3. **Ordering Activities**

Let's learn how we can use these steps to alter our life's focus in ways that empower us, increasing satisfaction in and giving more meaning to the tasks and activities we are involved in every day.

Defining Activities

We may have constructed the ideal mental picture of where we want to be but that picture is just a dream, until we act. So, how do we take clarity from inside our head and heart, and begin to construct our reality?

The first step is asking the question: "What type of activities should I be doing?"

Think of **defining activities** as outlining the main points of a term paper. Students would outline activities like attending class, studying, and socializing with friends. Accountants would define activities like learning new changes to the tax code, attending conferences or networking for business.

> *Our goal should be to look at the future state we desire and ask, "If I wanted _____ more than anything else, what would my daily activities need to be?"*

For example, I may want to learn to play the tenor saxophone. But what would be even better would be to play first chair tenor sax in the high school jazz band?

How badly do I want this? Am I willing to start aligning my actions toward that end?

Maybe I develop a boundary around my sax that I will not watch TV when I get home from school until I play my sax for one hour. Maybe that is enough to get me in the jazz band, but not first chair. Should I also limit myself to listening only to jazz on the way to school? I could also pull some other jazz band friends together and meet every day to learn and play new jazz pieces.

From the outside, it looks like I am just committed to jazz. But I will have more than commitment; I will also have boundaries I developed to help me achieve the result I desire.

We must align our boundaries with clarity to increase our likelihood of success, not decrease it. Light is truth and if we ignore it, we will fail. The greater the clarity, the stronger the boundary. The weaker the clarity, the more careful we must be when setting strong boundaries.

~ Align with Light and Focus ~

Think of our clarity discussion about light, focus, and frame. All three of those makeup clarity. Boundaries construct "focus" into our actions. However, without relying on the clarity revealed by light and frames, we can construct boundaries that destroy our lives and businesses.

We have talked about substance or alcohol abuse. What happens when we gain clarity in our lives and develop boundaries that construct a future clean of alcohol? We stop hanging out with friends who go to bars. They are still our friends, but we can't spend time with them when they are drinking. We don't go to bars. Drinking is not an option.

What do boundaries look like in someone with substance abuse, but without the "light" of clarity? Someone who cannot see a future clean of alcohol or drug addiction doesn't hang out with friends and family who tell them they need help. They don't want to be chastised, so they distance themselves from those people and only hang out with people who drink. They hang out in bars more than any other place.

Both individuals have set boundaries. One based on the light gained from clarity, and one without light. One moves toward a future self that is free of the problem; the other stagnates and blindly moves toward destruction. That is the power of boundaries.

In business, it is no different. We are cursed with a limited point of view. Sometimes we cannot see what is happening in the world around us and we make mistakes.

Remember our Blockbuster Video? At its peak, Blockbuster was worth over 5 billion dollars. Then Netflix began sending DVDs by mail to customers and set up a business model that had no late fees. Not long after Netflix, Redbox started opening kiosks across the country. Looking back, Blockbuster should have been losing sleep the minute they heard of either of these competitors. However, that is not at all how they perceived the threats.

In 2000, Reed Hastings, the founder, and CEO of Netflix, flew to the Blockbuster headquarters in Dallas, Texas. He asked the CEO of Blockbuster if they would be interested in a partnership. The idea was that Netflix would run Blockbuster's brand online and Blockbuster would promote Netflix in its stores. Hastings got laughed out of the room (Satell, 2014)[19].

Blockbuster saw no reason to do business with Netflix. They didn't help competitors—they crushed them. They had an opportunity to buy Netflix for 50 million dollars. Instead, they chose to ignore them and continue doing business as usual.

Fast forward, and Netflix is worth over 28 billion dollars, and Blockbuster filed for bankruptcy in 2010. They set boundaries, too. They drew a line in the sand and built great walls around their city – DVD in-store rentals. The only problem was people were searching outside of stores for their videos and getting them from Redbox and Netflix.

Blockbuster could have seen this shift in customer desire and need, and could have responded with flexibility and growth, but instead, the company refused to look to see if their clarity matched reality, and they became entrenched. **Their boundaries were strong but based on poor clarity.**

So, what is the result of poorly-set business boundaries? Bankruptcy. It didn't matter how efficient Blockbuster was at renting DVDs; they had constructed walls around a city that people were leaving. Ultimately, **they were protecting an abandoned city.**

~ Align with Frames ~

We discussed how to align our boundaries with light and focus from our Living Visual, but what about our frames?

Our frames reinforce and energize our boundaries. Frames are small distortions that are built into our worldview.

We discussed the dangers and effects of frames in Pillar I: Seek Clarity. Our frames help us describe the way the world works as **we** see it. So, when we look at our lives, businesses and the world around us and set boundaries, we must be careful.

Consider the example of the little girl who did not want to be in a room with a man, regardless if other people were in the room or not. She had set some very strong boundaries and it was easy to understand why. She had been severely hurt by a man. She needed to develop boundaries for protection so, in her little mind, she said: Men are bad. Don't be around men.

Unfortunately, such a tremendously limited worldview, using such strong boundaries, could make it difficult for this little girl to be happy in a world full of men she is trying to avoid.

When we set boundaries, we need an external check. We need some feedback on our thoughts and rationale. Are we developing boundaries out of fear, anger, complacency, pride, greed or other lower-order motives? Think back to the Mindful Quadrant. We build boundaries around what we harbor. Use the Mindful Quadrant to double check that your boundaries line up with your Living Visual.

Bring in outside opinions from your communities when you develop boundaries. If the boundaries you develop are accurate, you will get positive feedback and lots of encouragement, which will enhance your boundary.

Frames are the reason we all need coaches, mentors, counselors, advisors, consultants, parents, and friends for advice. We need a third party that is on the outside looking in to help us see reality clearly when we set boundaries.

~ Weak Boundaries ~

When I was in high school, I was involved in everything. On two separate occasions while playing basketball, I injured my left ankle. One of the injuries was so bad that the sports trainer said I had torn every ligament in my ankle and was just short of breaking it. The trainer suggested I see a doctor, have my ankle put into a boot to recover, and then rehab my ankle.

As an "invincible" high school athlete, I said "Okay" and walked out the door. But – I never saw a doctor, never got a boot, and never went to rehab. I wrapped my ankle without help from the trainer, and after a few weeks, did not have to limp and was back to playing ball. **What a stupid decision.**

Sometimes our decisions and weak boundaries have severe unintended consequences. In hindsight, I should have prioritized my ankle (personal health) and used stronger boundaries to protect that priority by limiting my activity, so I could reach my future self, the guy without a completely screwed up ankle and other joint problems years later.

Fast forward ten years.

I was married and playing with my wife in a co-ed softball tournament for fun. We had all joined the team to hang out every week with other young married couples that were our friends.

I hit the ball deep into the outfield and raced around the bases. As I crossed second base, my foot hit the back of the bag and threw my weight off balance. I came down on my left leg awkwardly, and "POP!" I remember, during what seemed like a slow-motion fall into short-stop, thinking, "Did I just break my leg?"

I face-planted, and quickly realized my leg was not broken. I had dislocated my hip.

The doctors were dumbfounded at my accident, and said it was an unusual, freak injury. It was a bad posterior dislocation and was out of place for several hours. I ended up having to wear a leg brace, walk on crutches, and not bend over past a 45-degree angle for almost three months. Then, I went through six months of rehab – and still, when it rains, I feel a slight pain in my hip.

I sound so old!

I found out later from a physical therapist that my left ankle had never completely healed. Apparently, for ten years I had unknowingly favored my right foot. The limp was so slight that it was not visible to me or anyone else. It further weakened my ankle, knees, and hip on the left side of my body. Rejecting proper treatment on my ankle contributed to the dislocating of my left hip ten years later.

Back then, something in my life changed and I did not respond properly. Instead, I came up with a mediocre quick-fix solution. It was good enough to keep me walking around school and kept me out of the doctor's office. But, it cost me a more painful injury later in life.

I had set up a weak boundary – a boundary that was good enough to make me feel good about things at the time, but didn't help me achieve the long-term results I truly needed. My weak boundaries did not flow from a Living Visual; they did not protect me or focus my efforts on recovery. They did just the opposite.

I was young and my experiences were limited to small injuries that recover quickly without medical attention or rehab. To operate at a higher level, to perform better, I should have trusted people with more experience, knowledge, and insight. Coaches, trainers, and doctors could have helped me set stronger boundaries and rehabilitated my ankle and kept my hip from popping out.

If we find ourselves slipping back into old habits that do not align with our Living Visual, we may be suffering the slow death of setting weak boundaries. The problem is harder to pinpoint because it is not immediately destructive.

Remember, we want to MOVE! toward our Living Visual and it may take some time. The bolder the boundary, the surer the footing with each step forward.

When people have no boundaries, it is easy to spot. They are a city without walls, and in one or more areas of their life, they are badly broken. People that set up weak boundaries may build a wall around their city, but it's either not high enough, not strong enough, or they leave holes in it.

What if we only let one marauder a night pass through the wall? In a whole city, that doesn't seem too bad. But eventually, that one marauder becomes ten or one hundred, and then one day catastrophe comes from inside the walls and you have no control. That is the problem with setting weak boundaries.

Strong boundaries are bolstered by bold actions.

Consider the pastor who shared the way he counseled men who had been unfaithful to their wives. He would sit across the table and ask them if they were serious about making things right.

If the man answered, "Yes," the pastor would ask for their cell phone. If they were brave enough to hand him their phone, the pastor would call their mistress, and then reveal that her lover had confessed. He would conclude the call by stating that the man would not speak with her again and was changing his number. Keeping the phone, he would then go with the man to the phone store to have his number changed. That is intense!

Can you imagine the gut-wrenching feeling in the room during that call? The pastor's process sounds harsh, but when you think about what he did, it makes sense.

The man had confessed to the affair and wanted it to end but had no walls or boundaries in place to face the woman and tell her it was over. In fact, his habits and routines were operating in opposition to his commitment to his wife. He needed help to set up the necessary boundaries to end the extra-marital relationship for good.

So, the pastor steps in and begins the re-organization of the man's life by building a bold boundary. The man doesn't have to make a lot of hard choices. The relationship is over. She can't even call him to ask what just happened.

Discipline and willpower are developed over time. They are not an unlimited resource, and it is a mistake to think that developing boundaries means exercising our discipline or willpower.

> *Boundaries reorient and redesign our lives around a new identity that needs to make fewer choices.*

Limiting Activities

So, how do our friends, who are volunteering at church, know when they are spending too much time helping their religious organization? They could argue that their work is in alignment with serving others and helping the church. Sounds noble, right? Sure, but not at the expense of other things, like a newborn or their health.

We easily can become overwhelmed and burned out doing good things. In the last section, we aligned our boundaries by defining the activities that were important for us to engage in, in order to produce our Living Visual. Those activities are what we know we want to pursue.

Now, we need to understand how to handle daily activities or opportunities that are presented to us. How do we know what to reject and what to pursue?

We need to use boundaries as a filter for all those great ideas, worthy causes, profitable opportunities, or favors that people ask us to participate in. We need a simple model to help us make decisions. How can we know that we have made a good decision and move?

Some decisions take a long time to process and work through. However, many times we become overwhelmed or fearful about making a decision. This cycle of worry and lack of definition can

make us feel like a hamster on a running wheel. We are expend-
ing all kinds of energy, but not going anywhere.

Setting proper boundaries can be achieved by passing our
activities through a series of boundary filters or checkpoint gates
in the walls we have built around our city.

If the activity is worthy, it will pass through the checkpoints,
and be added to the to-do list.

If it is not worthy, it is rejected at the checkpoints and not
allowed to enter our lives.

By using the checkpoint questions, we can be more confident
in our decisions and waste less time debating the merits of the
activity in our head.

The four checkpoint gates we use to limit the activities of our
lives are found in the following graphic.

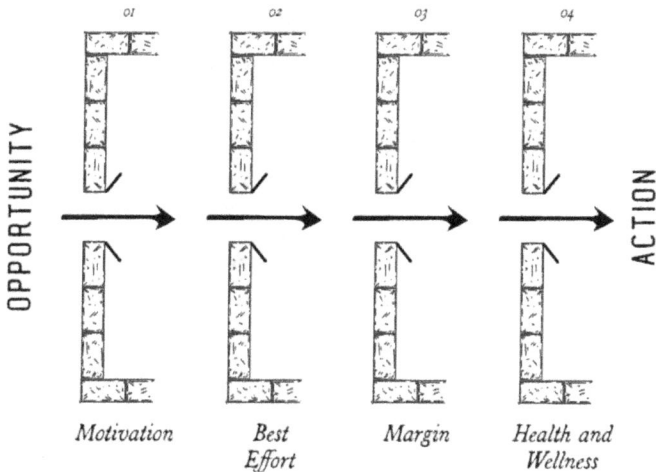

fig. 6
BOUNDARY CHECKPOINTS

In the diagram above, we see the name of the checkpoints that
help us decide what activities we need to pursue and what
activities to let go.

The *Motivation Checkpoint* limits the activities based on why we feel compelled to do the work.

The *Best Effort Checkpoint* limits our activities based on our level of commitment to the task or activity.

The *Margin Checkpoint* limits activities that we don't have enough time or energy to accomplish.

The *Health and Wellness Checkpoint* limits activities that do not promote our long-term health and wellness.

If an activity we are engaging in fails to pass through one or more of the checkpoints, then we should seriously re-consider its validity and importance to us.

The idea is similar to a teacher telling their class that they will take a test on all the material they have reviewed in the past month.

The class immediately asks the teacher to reveal specific sections, chapters, or topics that the test or exam will focus on. The students want to limit their studies to just the information that will be covered on the test.

When we limit our activity (studying), we increase our focus on the activities that have the biggest impact on achieving our goal (passing the test). When we pass on all the unnecessary activities in our lives, we can spend more time on meaningful activities or create space for reflection in our lives.

The questions below reflect how we should use the four checkpoint gates to keep from engaging in unnecessary activities.

~ Motivation Checkpoint ~

Why do I desire to do this activity?

Our desire to engage in a task should come from internal motivations like our beliefs, core values, convictions, mission, purpose, goals, objectives, and especially, our Living Visual.

If not, we risk adding tasks, because someone else wants us to do them. We feel pressure to please our parents or in-laws, friends, or siblings, so we end up adding tasks that create more stress and anxiety than if we just said "no."

As stated at the beginning of the chapter, if you are confused about what you should be doing, you need more clarity. The stronger the clarity, the stronger the boundaries we can develop around it. When we feel like we are progressing toward something that we see is valuable, we gain energy.

Imagine the marathon runner who turns the corner and sees the finish line a mile ahead. The clarity of the approaching finish line increases the drive and internal energy as the runner moves through the last mile.

~ Best Effort Checkpoint ~

Can I commit my best effort to this task?

If I heard the saying once, I heard it a thousand times growing up: "If a job is worth doing, it is worth doing well."

Sometimes, we have a task or direction we are motivated to pursue. However, we are not willing to put our best effort to the task. The lack of effort is a signal that our heart is not in it.

Maybe we are motivated to become a brain surgeon, because we like the title or the pay. No matter how motivated we are by the sound of being a brain surgeon, if we are not willing to put our best effort into 11 years of medical school and residency after college, we really don't want to do what it takes to be a brain surgeon.

Although this is an extreme example, we allow ourselves to do the same thing with smaller tasks every day. If we choose to do something, we must believe it is worth doing well and put our best efforts toward completing it.

Why do we need to focus on tasks that we can commit our best effort to?

We are all unique beings that have been given tremendous gifts. Why waste them by lack of focus or not engaging your whole self? Why not use those gifts in ways that add value to the world?

Like an artist who paints an original work and signs his name to it, living in our strengths gives us the ability to create things that will have our unique stamp.

~ Margin Checkpoint ~

Is this activity something that I have enough time and energy in my life to accomplish?

We all experience urgent matters that require immediate attention. Our kids start throwing up in the middle of the night. Our boss informs us that a deadline just moved up two weeks. Our parents have a car accident and are taken to the hospital.

These are situations that are both urgent and important.

However, many times requests may be urgent, but NOT important. "Please, please, please, PLEASE, Daddy, can I have this sucker!" at the register. Desperately urgent, not so important.

The Margin Checkpoint is where we take time to process if the task or activity is really something that we can do with the spare time and energy we have.

As our lives ebb and flow, this can shift from no margin to lots of margin and back again. Single parents don't have a lot of margin. Empty nesters can have so much margin that they don't know what to do with it.

Seasons of life will dictate how tasks and activities flow through the Margin Checkpoint, and that is perfectly normal.

~ Health and Wellness ~

How does this task or activity affect my long-term mental, emotional, and physical health and wellness?

We build playgrounds for kids at school, then build a fence around them.

Why?

Because we are telling our kids that everything within the fence is where they are free to play. The fence is in place to eliminate a child's decision between walking out into the road to get his ball or calling an adult. We remove the choice, and the risk.

Our mental and emotional wellness is important, too.

Watching a show on television to disconnect after a long day at work may help our mental or emotional state. Great stories are so powerful! However, watching television all night, at the expense of connecting with family and friends or working out, may not line up with your Living Visual.

Run activities through the Health and Wellness Checkpoint. Does this activity help me or not? If the answer is no, build a boundary to keep you from engaging in it or consuming time on something that is keeping you from moving.

The Health and Wellness Checkpoint does not eliminate every activity that may cause us hardship or stress.

To achieve our Living Visual, we may need to take on activities that are tough or require sacrifice. If we are sacrificing for something we know is important, we may continue the activity regardless of its negative effects on our wellness or health. We sacrifice something that is valuable to us for something that is more valuable to us.

The main objective of the last checkpoint is meant to keep useless activities that hurt our health and wellness out of our lives.

The Health and Wellness Checkpoint is also meant to make sure you think about *what* you are sacrificing.

Short-term loss of sleep to accomplish our Living Visual may be required and could be tolerated. However, if you go years with too little sleep and develop health problems, how does that help you accomplish anything?

If more clarity is needed, take out a piece of paper and write a scale of 1-10 (1 is lowest, 10 is highest). Circle how meaningful the work or task is to you. Next, circle the number that correlates to the level of sacrifice.

Sense of Meaning   1 2 3 4 5 6 7 8 9 10

Level of Sacrifice   1 2 3 4 5 6 7 8 9 10

Which number is higher? If the sacrifice is greater than the meaning, it may not be a good idea.

Think back to our friends who were being asked to volunteer for everything. We suggested they focus on activities they could do well, commit to doing them with excellence, and let all the other opportunities go. They also picked volunteer activities that fit into their schedule and were flexible enough to work around the needs of a newborn baby. Other people in their church had skills and gifts and needed to take on some of the other volunteer activities.

By asking ourselves the questions above and comparing them to our daily tasks, we can begin to see which and how many activities are unnecessary in our lives.

Our friends used the same checkpoint gates to better navigate what activities to volunteer for and what activities to let go. They gained more focus and margin to spend on meaningful activities in their church, while also maintaining proper boundaries around their family.

What activities are you involved in that would be stopped by one or more of the checkpoint gates?

Ordering Activities

In 1998, social psychologist, Roy Baumeister, published research that showed how people's willpower was not unlimited and could be depleted.[20]

Our self-discipline may be more like a muscle than we realize, and the more often we exercise our willpower, the more likely it will be that we run out when the next temptation strikes.

In Dr. Baumeister's test, he set a plate of warm cookies and a bowl of radishes in front of participants. He asked one group to enjoy the delicious cookies and the other group to resist eating the cookies, and instead eat radishes.

After eating cookies or radishes, he gave both groups a problem to solve that would require multiple attempts.

The group that resisted the cookies logged about 8 minutes, with 19 attempts. The group that ate the cookies logged about 18 minutes, with 34 attempts.

The group that resisted the cookies had much less self-discipline available to help in solving the problem; whereas, the group who ate the cookies had more self-discipline available.

Ordering our physical lives helps reinforce the strength of our emotional and spiritual lives (and vice versa). If we order the physical activities of our lives to reflect what is most important to us, it reduces the need to expend valuable willpower.

If our reserves of willpower are full, when we are tempted to get off track and cross over a boundary we developed, we easily resist.

Conversely, if we have little clarity or set skimpy boundaries in our physical lives, we are required to exert our willpower every day to keep from making poor choices, until we end up depleting our supply of willpower and finally give in.

The people who resisted the cookies in Dr. Baumeister's test lost the inner drive and willpower to solve mental problems.

> *We order our physical, emotional, and spiritual lives to minimize the willpower required to achieve our Living Visual.*

For example, if you have a problem with too much credit card spending, you may think: "I will only go to the mall and use my credit card on Fridays and only buy things I *really* need."

Watch out! Going to the mall with a credit card, with the intent of making a *few* purchases is poor ordering of physical habits if there is a history of lacking self-control.

How can someone order their physical life so they won't have to choose how to use their credit card?

Drum roll . . . cut up the card!

That is a bold boundary. Now, you don't have to decide if you need to buy something on your credit card, because you don't have one. Will spending money be more inconvenient? Maybe. Will you sleep better at night knowing you have control of your money, and don't have credit card bills looming over your head? Absolutely.

Now we have learned that boundaries aren't so bad, after all.

Remember to keep the proper perspective: *when we only see the boundaries we feel restricted, but when we see what they produce we feel free.*

When we can Align, Limit, and Order we realize all the benefits proper boundaries afford. So, take the time to think about whether there are tasks or activities in your life that need to come to an end.

Chapter 7

Barriers vs. Boundaries

What stands in the way becomes the way.

– Marcus Aurelius

I almost did not choose the word "boundary" to describe Pillar II because of the negative connotation often associated with the word. Why does the word "boundary" get such a bad rap?

I believe it comes from the idea of separation. We associate boundaries as a separation between one thing and another. Life shouldn't be about separating people and things, but bringing things together, right?

The real culprit in the negative connotation is mistaking *barriers* for *boundaries*. What is the difference?

Boundaries are something **we** build and can take down or change when needed. Barriers are set directly in our way by something external, limiting our movement and blocking us from achieving our Living Visual.

Is something or someone keeping me from moving toward my ideal state or narrowing my focus toward it? If so, it is not a *boundary*, it is a *barrier*.

Barriers give boundaries a bad name.

How do we deal with barriers in our life, considering they come in all different shapes and sizes?

They can be political opposition, physical limitations, geographical, or something as simple as gravity. Barriers may be big things like an ocean or a mountain that is insurmountable. They may also be smaller like a barricade of cops in the movies that are in between the modern-day Bonnie and Clyde trying to escape to freedom with their money.

In this book, we don't have time to unpack all the different barriers in our lives and the strategies to overcome them. But, we do need to *ask ourselves about the probability or possibility of overcoming the barrier before us.*

Is our Living Visual possible with the barriers obstructing our path?

Let's look at some examples and common themes of people who have successfully overcome big barriers in their lives.

Timing is Everything

When John F. Kennedy became President of the United States in 1961, the cold war was of great concern to the American people. Increasing and aggravating that concern was the Soviet Union's successful launch of the Sputnik satellite into space. The Soviets followed that amazing feat by sending the first man into space. The United States was falling behind in the space race against a formidable enemy.

So, in 1962, President Kennedy made a speech at Rice University in Houston, Texas proclaiming that the United States had deter-mined to put a man on the moon, and bring him home safely, by the end of the 1960s. He asked the US Congress to approve 5.4 billion dollars for the development of the necessary equipment.[21] When we calculate the inflation rate since 1962, it would be like a President Trump asking Congress for over 44 billion dollars!

What **barriers** did JFK face? First and easiest to identify were the financial barriers. Imagine needing to raise 5.4 billion dollars to start your business?

Second were the political obstacles. What would it look like if the venture failed and the US fell further behind the Soviets? In the eyes of the public, the Democrats credibility would be damaged for wasting all that money on a failure.

Third, and biggest, were the engineering obstacles; building a craft that could handle the physical challenges of the atmosphere of earth and the moon, while also keeping human cargo safe. Inserting humans into the heat and cold, lack of oxygen and desolation of the moon had never been attempted. How many calculations would be required to make it possible?

We would be mistaken if we assumed that JFK just had a dream one night and thought to himself, "I believe we should go to the moon." His actions and speech were not based on a dream or some theoretical vision. He based them on a multitude of discussions with experts, who were very familiar with the barriers to putting a man on the moon. Before JFK made his famous moon speech at Rice University, he presented his idea to Congress, and asked for funding. Here is an excerpt from his speech:

"Since early in my term, our efforts in space have been under review. With the advice of the Vice President, who is Chairman of the National Space Council, we have examined where we are strong and where we are not, where we may succeed and where we may not. Now it is time to take longer strides-time for a great new American enterprise-time for this nation to take a clearly leading role in space achievement, which in many ways may hold the key to our future on earth.

"I believe we possess all the resources and talents necessary. But the facts of the matter are that we have never made the national decisions or marshaled the national resources required for such leadership. We have never specified long-range goals on an urgent time schedule, or managed our resources and our time so as to insure their fulfillment."

Kennedy had been looking into the space program since early in his term. He was also given counsel on where the space program was strong and where it was not strong. He knew the limits of the program based on his conversations with experts, who held deep knowledge about the United States' capabilities. Then, after gathering all the data, he concluded that the **barriers** between the earth and the moon could be overcome by developing the needed technologies and applying the focus of necessary national resources.

He was also in the right place at the right time.

What if Kennedy had become president in 1850 and had the same vision? He may have been run out of office. He would have been called a dreamer, instead of a visionary.

No matter how badly he wanted to or how much money the government threw at the project in 1850, they would not have reached the moon in eight years or even eighty. The resources were just not available to overcome the biggest barrier to the moon: gravity.

Does the opportunity cost more money than is found in the bank account? What technical skill or abilities are required to accomplish the vision? What are the physical requirements?

All these questions play into overcoming barriers in our path.

When we see barriers in our path, we have to **take time to understand the barrier** and what it will take to push through, jump over, or go around. If we have the resources, skill, and experience, then we can apply focus, just like JFK, and charge the barrier.

Requires Risk

When we charge an obstacle or a barrier, it requires us to take a risk. Whenever we take a risk, we make assumptions and move in a direction that we believe will produce a positive result.

However, we move knowing that there is a chance that the result could be negative or out of our control.

How would you like to be the "lucky" guy picked to be strapped to a massive missile and blown 240,000 miles into space, and then asked to land in a spot the size of a football field?

It is easy to say: Me! Me! now that we know "lucky" made it back alive. But, what a tense situation for the first guy to blast through all the barriers that had separated mankind from the moon since the beginning of history!

Entrepreneurs consistently question and push barriers. They want to construct new systems that help customers achieve something they couldn't do before or buy something for less.

It is exhilarating to tackle barriers, but it's also risky. Launching startups is a risky investment, since some overcome the barriers they set out to beat, while others fail miserably.

Don't be afraid of barriers in life. Just seek to understand them and the risks associated with barreling through them. What could life look like if we break through? How much could it cost to be successful (in time, money and effort)?

> **Once we know the risks, we can decide to work around the barrier, break through it, or wait for better timing.**

Charge the Barrier

Marcus Aurelius was the last of the five Great Roman Emperors. He was very successful and ruled for almost 20 years. During his reign, he wrote a book called *Meditations*, where he articulates his philosophy on barriers. There are several translations of Book 5, Section 20, but one of my favorite translation reads:

*"Our actions may be impeded, but there can be no impeding our intentions or dispositions. Because we can accommodate and adapt. The mind adapts and converts to its own purposes the obstacle to our acting. The impediment to action advances action. **What stands in the way becomes the way."***

This quote ties together a lot of what we have discussed. We don't have control over barriers, but we can control our response to them. If overcoming the barrier is central to achieving our Living Visual, get ready and hold on.

The barrier becomes the way.

Our greatest challenges become the necessary path to achieve our greatest desires.

Don't run from it. Embrace it!

Pillar II Review

We discovered in Pillar II that Boundaries flow out of our Living Visual. When we start with a clear picture, we can gain focus by organizing our life around achieving that end.

We also discovered six benefits we receive when we set proper boundaries in our life.

1. Freedom to Focus
2. Protect Our Priorities
3. Define Distinction
4. Reinforce Our Roles and Responsibilities
5. Protect Our Interest
6. Control the Flow

Boundaries are indispensable to movement. So, we learned a strategy to set proper boundaries in our lives. We learned to **align** the boundaries with clarity, **limit** the boundaries to four main areas in our lives, and **order** our lives in a way that reduces the need to constantly make decisions and exert willpower.

By aligning, limiting, and ordering, we can now save ourselves the time and mental anguish of constantly second-guessing every decision we make.

Finally, we discussed the contrast between boundaries and barriers. Boundaries are walls that we build around our lives to enhance our movement. Barriers are external impediments to our movement. Barriers are those things that stand in the way between where we are and where we want to be.

Pillar II Challenge:

Are there areas in your life or work that feel out of control?

Before moving on to Pillar III, devote some time to reflect and understand how you can set proper boundaries to increase your focus.

When you do this, do you feel any of the following symptoms?

1. Anxiety
2. Analysis Paralysis (overwhelmed at all the decisions you need to make)
3. Confusion
4. Fear of losing control
5. Burnout
6. Lack of impact

If so, take some comfort in knowing that setting proper boundaries will dramatically improve your life. As you begin to align yourself toward where you want to be, you will discover what activities are stealing your time, but not moving you toward your Living Visual.

You may find that it's time to practice saying NO to a few things, so you can say YES to the most important things.

You can do it!

Pillar III

Elevate Accountability

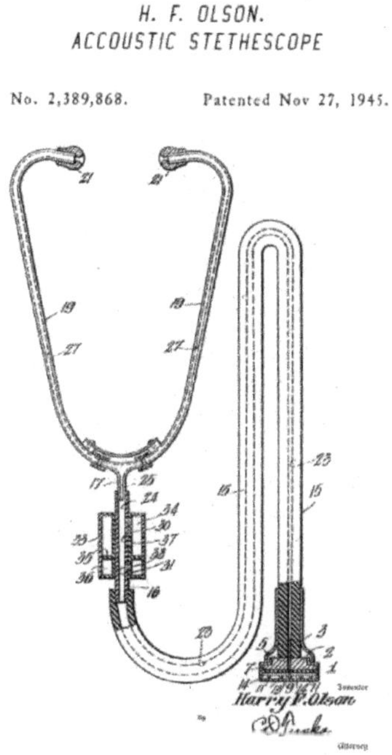
H. F. OLSON.
ACCOUSTIC STETHESCOPE
No. 2,389,868.
Patented Nov 27, 1945.
Harry F. Olson

fig. 7

The enemy of accountability is ambiguity.

– Patrick Lencioni

To be accountable, *we have to own something*. We can't be held accountable for the hurricane that wiped out our neighborhood or the recession that has taken a toll on our business. Those things are out of our control.

When we own something, we are in control and give an account of the results we produce with it. We can't delegate it. We can't blame the results on someone else or hand the work to a third party to finish.

So, what is the most important thing we own? **Our responses**.

Ask yourself: "What else can I do to respond to my circumstance or situation and achieve the results I desire?

The quote from Patrick Lencioni is a perfect segue from Boundaries. Where there is ambiguity, interpretation, or multiple answers, there is little accountability. Just as boundaries are developed from clarity, accountability is elevated from our boundaries.

Clarity answers the big questions, like where we are going.

Boundaries, in turn, are like the white lines painted on the road to keep us from driving into oncoming traffic or off a bridge.

Accountability is like road signs on a highway, gauges on our car, and police officers in our figurative rear-view mirror.

> When we Elevate Accountability, we measure the pace of our movement, how efficiently we are moving, and if we are moving in the correct direction toward our desired destination.

Accountability increases our performance because it measures our performance related to our goals. It also forces us to address issues and distractions that can derail our movement.

We gain something very important when we start measuring results: awareness. We may think we are doing a great job, but only when we start tracking the results do we know where we stand.

For this reason, we must "Elevate" our desire to hold our responses accountable.

When we Elevate Accountability, we hold our responses accountable for creating the marriages, businesses, financial stability, or future selves that we desire.

If we do not hold our responses accountable, we lose the momentum we need to keep moving within our boundaries toward our destination. We are left with no control, a ship without a rudder.

The Problem with Ideas

People who are not accountable do not look at the results. Sometimes we get wound up in an idea, and then get wound up in how good the idea makes us feel, and then, the results don't really seem so important, because it all just seems so great.

All that matters to us is that we feel good about associating and identifying with our idea. Our intent is pure and noble. Honest! But, doesn't something feel a little wrong about that?

It is possible to confuse an idea we want to move toward with the *reality* we are creating.

There is a vast chasm between someone's intent and someone's impact.

You may think it doesn't seem like a big difference, but we make huge mistakes moving toward an idea versus creating a new reality. Reflect on the consequences of pursuing ideas and examples will start to emerge.

We all know friends who were so desperate to fall in love or get married that they rushed into a relationship. They were moving toward the **idea** of love or marriage, not the reality of love and marriage. The reality of marriage is that poor choice in a spouse may result in infidelity, arguments, abuse, and divorce. Even with a fantastic spouse, all marriages will be tested and only the ones that can thrive in the "best of times" and survive the "worst of times" will make it.

Ideas are easy. They are all unicorns and rainbows. They may be the picture of the perfect family, the perfect kids, the perfect job, the perfect house, the perfect marriage, or the perfect career.

Reality looks a lot more like hard work. Plus, chasing ideas creates all kinds of chaos in our lives.

We must work hard to separate the idea from the reality.

At the beginning of the book, I told you how I had to make a choice about moving to Nashville with my wife so I could work toward becoming a professional singer/songwriter. Thoughts and ideas of being on TV and on stage in front of thousands of fans, receiving awards, and making millions of dollars could make a move in that direction very tempting. However, that was just one small, highly improbable frame of the total picture of becoming a professional singer/songwriter living in Nashville.

To make the right decision, we needed information based on reality. So, I talked to a lot of people in the industry. We looked hard at the lives of friends already in the music industry in Nashville.

Once we felt like we had clarity on what the life of a singer/songwriter would be, we compared it to what we wanted our life to look like.

The big question became: **could I create the life I wanted** by being a singer/songwriter?

If the idea matched my Living Visual and helped me create the future self I wanted to be, it was time to move. If not, no amount of glitz and glamor would be enough to make me happy.

Accountability separates the *idea* of a professional singer/songwriter from the *reality* of the life of a professional singer/songwriter.

In the end, we decided not to move to Nashville. It was a conscious and intentional decision. We were clear that the reality of that move was not the reality we wanted to create with our family. The decision is one I do not regret. In fact, it is one of my most treasured decisions *because* it was so intentional.

I am not suggesting that a career as a professional musician is bad. Nor am I suggesting that people in the music industry are not living fulfilled lives. We still have friends in the business and music is still a very big part of our family.

My point is simply that **we must move toward the reality that is in alignment with the future we are trying to create.**

Don't move toward an *idea* that seems right for everyone either. Our purpose is not for everyone, only us. Relish your accountability. Welcome personal responsibility.

It's the difference between liking the idea of being a NASCAR driver from our couch on Sunday afternoon and going down to the local dirt track and signing up.

We don't **do** ideas. We hold ourselves accountable to create future realities.

How do we know what we know?

Since the beginning of the book, we have followed a natural path of thinking; built a Living Visual that describes where we are and where we want to go; and have created proper boundaries to increase our focus to that end.

Now we know that accountability is important, but we still may not understand how to become accountable.

Christopher Columbus is attributed with the quote, "Following the light of the sun, we left the Old World." He had no idea where his journey would end – *but he knew what he knew*. He knew he was headed toward the light, leaving the Old World, and had set his mind to find the New World.

How do we know what we know?

It took a lot for Columbus to even get out of the harbor. He had to raise substantial money, find a crew, secure a ship, and prepare for a voyage with no known endpoint. Then, take a big gulp and get on the ship.

Sounds crazy, right? It also sounds a lot like how we describe today's entrepreneurs.

Columbus was clear on his mission. He knew as much as he could before he left. He had a plan.

So, how was he accountable?

Columbus was not only accountable to return with gold or treasures for the King and Queen of Spain; he was accountable to lead his crew safely to the New World.

Every day he asked himself:

Are we on course?
How much food do we have?
Who is sick? How much further can we make it?
Should we change course?
Should we turn back?

Asking great questions to life's everyday challenges is how we know what we know. We can begin *responding* to reality as it relates to the end goal.

Let's look at accountability and discuss how we can build a strong foundation, how we practice the art of accountability, and what we should produce when we Elevate Accountability.

Chapter 8

Building a Foundation

To end with certainty, we must begin with doubting.

– Stanislaus

———————

Just like with a house or skyscraper, the foundation of account-ability is critical to the strength and stability of the end result.

When we build a house, we begin with the end in mind. The depth and shape of the foundation perfectly match the size of the structure we are constructing. Our foundation is something we can measure, even before the house is built.

The following three sections describe the three most important components necessary to lay a strong foundation and to begin to Elevate Accountability in our lives.

Standards

The first foundational component necessary to Elevate Accountability is to create *Standards*. To create accountability in ourselves and others, we must have clarity about the standards we hope to meet. Remember: *Ambiguity is the enemy of accountability.*

If you don't know what you are aiming for, how do you know when you have hit the mark?

In business, it may be profitability or production speed or quality – or all three. In ministry, it may be community service, membership, training, or donations. In a career, it may be job choices that comply with the standards you have set for your life.

Accountability requires us to be responsible for moving toward the standards we set.

The great news is: you have already done the work! The heavy lifting for standards happens when you are defining your Living Visual. If you have successfully defined what you want to pursue, it makes accountability possible. Without clarity, how do you know what to be accountable to?

For the past eighteen years, a local nonprofit organization in upstate South Carolina, Homes of Hope (www.homesofhope. org), has done amazing work; building homes for people in need, while also running a rehabilitation program for men working through their recovery from drug and alcohol addictions. Of the 293 graduates from the men's development program, most have lived in the same home in Greenville, SC. And of the nearly 600 homes built for needy families, the majority went up in just a few counties in South Carolina.

From its inception, Homes of Hope has had a tremendous impact on raising individuals and families out of poverty and helping them achieve their goal of homeownership.

The story behind this successful endeavor represents the first element of our foundation: **Standards**.

Homes of Hope began out of a dire need in the community.

A family lost their home and all their possessions in a fire. Desperate for help, they heard of a local businessman, Tim, a mobile home salesman, who might help them find a temporary place to stay. The family approached Tim and asked if there was anything he could do to help them find shelter for their family.[22]

Part of Tim's business included buying old mobile homes and renovating them. He renovated one of the mobile homes, moved it to their lot for no charge and let the family stay there until they got back on their feet.

Several nights later, Tim woke up at 3 am, like a lightning bolt went off in his mind, and he couldn't sleep.

The next morning, he called his controller, Don, into his office and stated, "Don, I woke up in the middle of the night and God gave me instructions."

Don listened carefully as Tim passionately described how he was told that he was supposed to use his business to help provide housing for people in the community. He was supposed to call the new non-profit Homes of Hope.

Homes of Hope was to have a very specific mission and has kept the same three founding principles throughout: Faith, Focus, and Favor.

Don was enthusiastic about the idea and Tim assigned to him the task of managing the new organization.

In the beginning, the staff would go down and pick up guys from a local rehab center and give them work helping remodel the mobile homes. Then, the remodeled homes would go to families in the area who needed housing.

Don would later recall that when they first started, they got a few things right, but a lot of things wrong.

All went well for the first year. Tim was supporting the non-profit by donating $40,000 a month from his business proceeds to pay the employees and buy the materials needed to build and remodel the homes.

Then in 2000, a year into the venture, the mobile home market evaporated.

Tim asked Don to lunch one day and gave him some difficult news.: "I am out. I can't fund Homes of Hope anymore because my business is through, but you have been running it, so it is yours."

Tim fully expected Don to throw in the towel and quit, but was floored by Don's response, "Well, let's see what God does."

Don then went back and told his entire staff he could no longer pay them. The staff looked at Don and said no problem; we believe that it will all work out. We are staying with you.

For the next two years, Don worked for Homes of Hope without taking a salary. He lived a powerful example of true conviction. Some of the stories of how he and his family were taken care of during that time are nothing short of a miracle.

All five original staff members stayed and made it through the difficult season that followed the contraction of founder funding. The commitment of Don and the rest of the team through the early years helped them gain more clarity on how to manage the organization.

After reviewing their early results, Don decided to change their approach to ensure they attained and maintained the standard initially set for their project: **not to just give a house or job to someone, but to change their life.** As we Elevate Accountability, it is important to set clear standards for ourselves or our organizations. These standards inform our understanding of our success or shortcomings as we create movement. In this example, Homes of Hope set a standard for changing lives, not only providing housing. Affordable housing is the means, but changing lives is the end.

How did Homes of hope apply the standard and change lives? They had recently been given a house in Greenville for remodeling and decided that when it was completed, the men who graduated the local addiction program could live there for a year after graduating. The home was christened the "Gideon House."

Today, when men show up at the Gideon House, they have access to classes, through a partnership with the local community college, in an area of construction they enjoy, plus transportation. When they are not in class, they help build houses without pay for Homes of Hope, which further develops their marketable skills.

When they graduate at the end of the year, they have a certificate from the local technical college and experience. Every graduate is hired by local contractors and employers and most are well above starting pay because of Homes of Hope's reputation in the community.

Homes of hope uses the construction of affordable housing to help men overcome addition and build marketable skills which give them hope and opportunity. They not only provide affordable housing, but they also offer financial training and other programs to new homeowners to make sure that the experience of moving into a new home goes far beyond signing a lease or mortgage. The **Standard** guides the movement and gives Homes of Hope a clear result to measure against. *What Standards have you set in your life that help inform your movement?*

How are the leaders of Homes of Hope accountable?

Tim was so shaken by his middle-of-the-night experience that he immediately began funding the organization. He did exactly what he was told, down to the name of the non-profit. He felt accountable.

After taking over the operations of the company, Don felt accountable to continue the work of the organization even after the funding disappeared almost overnight. He worked hard, did fund-raising, and did not take a salary for two years so he could pay staff and continue helping those in need.

The staff was accountable to the mission of Homes of Hope, too. They went without pay and reached out to friends and family for support, while continuing to run the organization.

Can you imagine showing up at your job for two years with no pay? Working long hours, sweating in the heat, freezing in the cold, and at the end of the week not going home with a dime?

Many people at this point might say, "Those guys at Homes of Hope are crazy."

Maybe! But the results of their work and the impact on the surrounding community doesn't seem like the work of crazy people.

Tim and Don had something in common from the beginning: Clarity — very intense clarity. Strong clarity and a powerful desire to move, helped Tim and Don Elevate Accountability. They lived with an intense focus on their mission and the standards they set at the very beginning.

Even after 20 years of running Homes of Hope, Don still gets emotional describing all the changes in people's lives (including his) along the way.

How did Homes of Hope create an organization with a culture of accountability?

When the men arrive at the Gideon House, they have successfully completed an addiction rehab program. They don't have a job. They may have strained relationships with their family. They have not been trustworthy, due to the power of their addiction.

However, what they *do* have is the clarity that they want to change, which means they can accept and benefit from living in a culture of accountability.

Homes of Hope helps the men set boundaries in their life to help keep them from falling back into drug use. They help change the men's pattern of behavior from users and abusers to producers and givers.

It is not an easy task for Homes of Hope or the men, who all live in the same house and are responsible for each other.

Every morning they are visited by Homes of Hope staff who take them through a daily devotion, encourage them, and take attendance. Then, it is off to work, building houses for Homes of

Hope or off to school to learn specific skills related to the construction industry.

The men know there are no second chances. Everyone in the addiction program is subject to random weekly drug testing, and if they are dismissed from Homes of Hope, they cannot get back in.

For a year, they work hard at a trade, earn money, learn about how to manage finances, receive positive attitude coaching, and, most of all, are given a chance to change their life.

Do the men in Homes of Hope Gideon House graduate angry because they are held accountable for their actions all year?

Nope.

They come out and say, "It changed my life." Families are healed, addictions are broken, lives are changed.

And it started with two men being accountable to a calling.

Reinforcement

The second foundational component necessary to Elevate Accountability is, *Reinforcement* of the *Standards*. Accountability rests on standards that we measure our progress against.

In the foundation example, different measurements would be taken for the foundation of a 2-story single family house versus a 120-story office building. The same is true with accountability. The measurements we take should reinforce the types of behavior that we want to produce.

Think about Homes of Hope. They don't want recently-sober men falling back into drug use.

So, how do they reinforce that using accountability?

Drug test often. That is good because you know *if* one of the men slip back into drug use, but it is not enough reinforcement to maintain the "no drug use" desire, which is why they keep the men busy.

They also measure hours worked, devotion attendance, and grades in school every week. If you are at work and school and meeting with mentors, then you have very little time to get involved with drugs. Measuring if the guys are at work, school and devotions is how Homes of Hope reinforces accountability, while working to change patterns of behavior in the lives of the men of Gideon House.

These metrics, in addition to the drug tests, reinforce the main objective of life change.

> **Reinforcing accountability means intentionally measuring certain routines that naturally produce the desired result if accomplished.**

The Homes of Hope example demonstrates how we reinforce our accountability on an organizational level, but it works on a personal level, too.

I am not a morning person. No matter how hard I try, it's a battle to rise and shine. For years, I traveled a lot for business and many times needed to catch a 6 am flight. Beyond measuring what time I had to wake up, I also set a time to be in bed, a time to turn off all electronic devices, and how early I worked out during the evening. These additional metrics helped keep me accountable and made it much easier to rise and shine at 4 am – as long as I hit those other targets first.

One important aspect of reinforcing measurements is that many times these routines are where our battle with discipline and willpower take place.

Rising at 4 am is non-negotiable, just like the Homes of Hope Drug Test. However, going to bed by 10 pm is not a **requirement** for getting up at 4 am. Turning off my phone 1 hour before bed is also not a requirement. But, going to bed early and turning off my phone promotes healthy sleep and sufficient rest, so it will be easier to rise early.

We may not always win the small battles of going to bed early or cutting off the phone, but if we win most of them, most of the time, it decreases the chance of oversleeping and increases the likelihood we will feel good in the morning.

When we want to reinforce certain behaviors, we should look to our boundaries. They tell us what types of actions and responses we should be doing; and more importantly, what we should **not** be doing.

It is important to know when we are close to breaking a boundary or begin operating outside a boundary. So, we need to think about what boundaries are in place and how to confirm we are operating inside of them.

For example, when you rent a U-Haul trailer, there is a hitch on the front of the trailer that is connected to your vehicle so it can pull the trailer.

The hitch is like a boundary that says the trailer must move in line with the vehicle.

In addition to the hitch, there are also (usually) two chains, one of either side of the hitch, that are also connected to the vehicle. The chains are there so that if the hitch breaks or comes loose, the chains keep the trailer connected to the vehicle, instead of rolling off into oncoming traffic.

The chains reinforce the boundary – the hitch.

Meaning

The last foundational component necessary to Elevate Accountability is understanding that our accountability is *meaningful*.

Meaningful accountability has a positive answer to the question: "Are our best efforts **able** to physically accomplish what we **want** to accomplish?"

> ✦ Accountability must be taken seriously. If our efforts are futile, we will not sustain our movement.

If our activities do not produce the results we want to achieve, then our activities are not meaningful. We should continually take a step back and ask: if we are successful in our activities, will we produce the result we wanted?

Could you imagine Christopher Columbus saying that same quote about heading toward the sun, as he climbed into a rowboat with two of his friends? It would be meaningless. They would barely make it out of the harbor.

In my early twenties, I was driving across Kentucky to a meeting with some water plant operators. I wanted to see if I could help them save money or achieve better water quality results.

It was my first time visiting plants in Kentucky and I soon learned not to be in a hurry. I also learned that folks in Kentucky love horses and telling stories (we have both in common).

One story I was told was so outlandish I couldn't believe it. But when I got back home and did some research, sure enough, it was true.

In Lawrenceburg, Kentucky, at about 3:15 p.m. on May 9th, 2000, a Wild Turkey bourbon storage facility caught fire.[23] The storage warehouse was seven stories tall and built of wood. It housed over 15,000 gallons of Wild Turkey bourbon stored in oak barrels and aged for almost 15 years.[24]

When it caught fire, barrels of bourbon started exploding and the entire building collapsed in just a few minutes. The bourbon, still on fire, ran down the hill toward the river, catching everything in its path on fire. During the disaster, local schools and businesses were closed, and people joked that the town was going to have Happy Hour down by the river!

Sadly, days later the alcohol content in the river fed the algae, which bloomed and grew, depleting the oxygen supply and killing all the fish in the river in a 28-mile dead zone. Locals said in some areas there were so many fish floating it looked as if you could walk across the river on them. Thankfully, the company paid over $250,000 to return the fish to the river and clean up the mess.

In between the storage warehouse and the river was a water plant, built down the slope from the warehouse. When the warehouse collapsed the liquid fire ran downhill – you guessed it – right toward the water plant. When the fire department showed up at the water plant to fight the fire, they found out some very disheartening news. *There was no fire hydrant.*

The small detail of the missing fire hydrant did not make the news. However, it did circulate through the water operators. You can bet many of the nearby plant operators went outside that day looking for a hydrant.

25

Luckily, the water plant had a small berm built up around the plant to level the ground for the water basins. The raised ground was the only thing that saved the plant. Fortunately, the water system had a two-day supply of water and was able to open the plant up before the water ran out. The picture above shows just how close the fire came to the water plant.

When engineers build a water plant, they are responsible for delivering water to the people in the surrounding area. And that is just what the Lawrenceburg Water Plant on the side of the Kentucky River did.

They had standards: provide clean water. They reinforced activities that produced clean water by training employees, locating the plant on a major river, and testing the quality of the water every day. Great.

But was the design of the water plant meaningful? If the engineers are accountable, what should they take account of? What should they have considered in great detail?

Any reasonable or potential problem, incident or catastrophe that could stop the plant from producing clean water!

In this case, the 15,000 gallons of liquid fuel sitting in a wooden barn on the hill above the water plant.

Accountability means you are able and responsible for giving an "account" of the performance and results. That is why it is important to pay close attention to **meaningful details**. Keep the main thing, the main thing. If the plant cannot produce water, then they have not achieved their performance goal.

As you approach creating movement in work or life, don't forget to lay the foundations of accountability. Remember that accountability needs to be anchored in some standard or calling. We do not wait until the results come in to find out how we did, we pro-actively design and measure our actions and responses in order to routinely produce our desired results.

Finally, we must focus on meaningful details and guard against being distracted by urgent or shiny things unrelated to our goals and objectives.

Chapter 9

Reviewing the Tape

Twice and thrice over, as they say, good is it to repeat and review what is good.

– Plato

Now that we have covered the foundations necessary for successful accountability, we can discuss the activity of "accounting."

In this chapter, we will understand how we should conduct the act of accounting for our performance.

The **three main activities** we will cover are **detaching, designing, and directing**. These three activities will show how we can use accountability to help us refine our efforts and ensure that our responses are producing our desired outcome.

Detach

When we think about the act of accounting, one word that does not naturally come to mind is *detachment*. But the truth is, to be truly accountable, we have to detach from the activity itself.

Detachment is taking stock of your actions or performance from outside of what you are doing. This may sound confusing or strange, but we see examples of detachment every day.

At the beginning of Pillar III, there is a picture of a stethoscope patent. Could you imagine sitting on the examination table, after putting on the uncomfortable paper-gown, and have the doctor walk in and ask: "Do you have an irregular heartbeat right now?"

You would probably check out and find another doctor, because you can't <u>hear</u> your heart beating in your chest!

Fortunately, the good doctor instead pulls out his trusty stethoscope, which is detached from your body, and gets a clear reading of your heartbeat.

You need perspective from outside.

Think about your favorite basketball team. Close your eyes and pretend you are at their biggest game of the year. It's a home game. The crowd is packed into the arena. It's loud. Really loud. You can smell the popcorn and hear the pep band in between the buzzer blasts. The game is close. The referees are making poor calls, in your opinion. The coach calls timeout and draws up a play. Then, as the team moves the ball, the coach is yelling at the players to make adjustments. After that, the referees make another bad call and the coach is all over them. He makes a couple of substitutions after glancing at the bench.

After the game is over, a news reporter grabs the star player and says, "What did you think of your performance tonight?" What does he say? Most of the time it depends on if the team won or lost. If they won, he/she says, "We played great!" If they lost, he/she says, "We just didn't play that well tonight."

Is the player right or wrong?

It depends. Maybe they did have the game of their life and won. However, the player has been so intimately tied to the performance and execution he/she has had no time to process what just happened. It's been all buzzers, cheering, lights, and pressure shots. The players are moving, executing and trying to stay off the bench!

How do we find out how the team really did?

We watch the tape. The tape doesn't lie. The coach sits down after the pep band stops playing and the crowd goes home; no longer yelling at players or referees. He and his staff sit silently in a dark room and turn on the recording of the game.

The coach has successfully **detached from the moment** to gain clarity through objectivity.

In the moment, things happen fast. In the moment, we don't see all the moving parts. We can't inspect the game from multiple angles. We are emotionally involved in the execution of our plans. It's blood, sweat and tears – and we **feel** it all.

That is why at the end of a win the player says: "We played great!" The player feels great, so he assumes they played great.

So, when we detach, we remove the emotion and the distortion it can cause. We start looking at the numbers. We start asking more difficult questions. Did I make the right substitution at the end of the game? Did we make the right adjustments after the half?

The tape doesn't lie. And after the coach watches the game from all angles and in slow motion, he can then say, based on the information he has gathered, that the team won, but played terribly. Conversely, the team may have suffered defeat, but the coach may see that the team played their best game of the year.

When we detach from our actions and execution, we can be more objective. We lessen the emotion tied to our efforts that blinds us to the reality of the situation.

When we are trying with all our might to accomplish something, the last thing we want to hear is: "You're doing it all wrong."

But, what if we *are* doing it all wrong?

When we Elevate Accountability, we must detach from the activity to objectively decide if our efforts are producing the desired result.

Detachment also gives us perspective. When we are in the moment, we can see our goal and become discouraged. If you are an achiever-oriented person, you may "feel" like your movement is progressing too slow or not at all. It is like a player in the example above who loses the game and is discouraged, because they feel like they did not play well, despite playing their best game of the season.

> ✵ **Detaching helps us enjoy the process, not just the result.**

One of the great Renaissance painters, Michelangelo, was commissioned to paint the ceiling of the Sistine Chapel. He painted the enormous work of art in three sections. He also designed special scaffolding for him to work from, because the ceiling was so high. It took four years of daily painting to finish the work.

After Michelangelo finished the first third of the ceiling, he had the scaffolding taken down, so the painting could be seen from the floor.

To Michelangelo's disgust, some of the details he had meticulously added into the work were not visible from the floor. It was too far away. It is said that in defeat, he left the Sistine Chapel and went back to his hometown. It took armed guards to bring him back to finish one of the greatest pieces of art in the world.

The last two-thirds of the ceiling was completed, but he learned from the first what level of detail was acceptable by distancing himself from it.

Our viewpoint is at a disadvantage when we are directly engaged in life, work, or moving. We see what is in front of our face and think we are dead on. Yet when we back up and see the full picture, we realize we were not moving in the right direction, after all.

When our nose is 6 inches from the ceiling, we have no way of knowing that our efforts are in vain.

Everybody knows someone who seems to fall into the same difficulties or re-live the same poor relationship or wind up in the same kinds of trouble again and again.

Maybe they complain about terrible dates yet continue to go to bars to meet people or haphazardly use dating apps. Or, maybe they complain of having no money or job, but continue to gamble or buy frivolous items or act irresponsibly at whatever job they have.

There are any number of 'maybe they . . .' possibilities, but in the end, these are people who allow emotion or impulse to drive what they do. They are blind to the well-worn path they are trotting along because they can't step aside and look at their situation from the outside. Emotion creates a huge blind spot and makes it difficult to be objective. They follow the feeling of "idea" versus the "reality" of their responses, as we talked about in the opening of Elevate Accountability.

Detachment helps us control our emotions and take the time to respond to the environment or situation; instead of mindlessly reacting to it. It is looking at the situation from the outside in and being able to use a *pre-determined response.*

Do you want to be an actor and move to New York City? Before you go, decide what you want your life to look like if you make it or if you don't. Develop your Living Visual around each path. Then give yourself a deadline. Tell yourself, "If I haven't been able to achieve some traction in 3 years I am leaving to pursue other work that gives me satisfaction." You give your dreams a shot and a deadline. Don't wait until you are in the grind going to auditions to decide when it is time to leave. Make it before your emotions and energies cloud your judgement.

Design

Another key to successful accountability is designing your responses and activities in a way that forces you to produce the desired performance or result.

In Chapter 8: Building a Foundation, we discussed the importance of understanding what measurements reinforce the behavior you want to produce. Similarly, we want the actual activities themselves to be tailored to eliminate the chance of non-performance.

Milliken & Company is a private corporation that is world-renowned for its production efficiency and workplace safety. Milliken is one of those companies that make tons of things you use every day, but you never realize they are part of that thing you're using.

For example, Milliken chemists are the ones who invented the ingredient that makes Tupperware™ clear. Yep, you would never know without opening the lid that the green beans lost in the back of your fridge were becoming a thriving science project, before Milliken. Their chemicals and products are everywhere.

When I was in college, I interned at Magnolia, one of Milliken's largest textile finishing plants. A finishing plant takes rolls of fabric and sends it through a process that adds color and other properties, like stain resistance, to the fabric.

The plant was enormous and I remember during orientation the manager telling us that it was the size of 19 football fields under one roof. Before the end of the summer, I had walked every inch of the plant many times.

When I was there they were clearing a section of the factory to make room for a new piece of equipment: the APEX finishing line. The machine was massive – 350 feet long and several stories tall.[26] It was also complicated; with parts that had extreme dry heat, color baths, scouring chemicals, steam, rollers, and all kinds of other bells and whistles. Millions of feet of fabric ran through it every month.

Could you imagine being in charge of running a machine that was as long as a football field?

It would have been easy for Milliken to hire an outside engineering firm that specialized in building this type of equipment, holding them financially accountable if it failed.

But Milliken took a different approach.

While they did hire the engineering firm, they brought in a handpicked team of executives, managers, mechanics, engineers, and floor workers to have input on the new design. They wanted everyone who would run the machine to also have input into how it was built.

After they began installation, Milliken put the mechanics who would work on the machine, if it ever broke down, on the installation team. The mechanics saw APEX from the inside out and how everything fit together.

They gave the mechanics, managers, and floor workers the ability to ask: "Is this right?" during installation. If part of the machine design did not make sense, it was changed immediately.

Finally, after installation, the floor workers and managers were tasked with making sure that everything was working properly and were given a punch list of items that should be corrected. While the punch list items were being completed, the floor team and managers were also tasked with writing an operational procedure manual for the APEX.

When the big day arrived to start APEX for the first time, Milliken was confident it would be successful.

Most companies would have asked the engineers and contractors who built the machine to start it up for the first time, then run it and train the employees. Not Milliken!

Instead, they asked the employees to start up the machine and show the engineers and contractors how to run it.

Milliken understood that it was not enough to hire an engineer and walk away. **They designed a plan that ensured their employees were intimately involved in every detail, so that when it was time to launch, there were no surprises.** The project was designed to be successful from the start.

Recently, I spoke with one of the former plant managers about the APEX project and we started talking about accountability.

He said that many companies he spends time with have employees who can't answer this very important question: **"How do you know you've had a good day?"**

He related that many employees would give such answers as: I finished my task early, I didn't get hurt, I didn't make a mess, my boss didn't yell at me. All revealing that they have set a low standard for accountability.

At Milliken, an employee would answer: "I had a good day because my machine only had 3 minor stops" or "I met my goal to have less than 0.3% off quality per day."

So, how do we know *we've* had a good day? How can we design our activities and responses to make sure we do?

I confessed in the last chapter that I am not a morning person and that I had to measure certain activities the night before in order to wake up feeling refreshed.

But, what if that wasn't enough?

What if I got to bed early and still hit the snooze button? What could I easily do to eliminate that option? How about if I put my alarm clock in the bathroom or on the other side of the bedroom, forcing me to get out of bed in order to silence the alarm?

Once I'm up, the likelihood I would get back in bed is very low. And there you have it – a wake-up routine designed to eliminate the possibility of over-sleeping.

Milliken designed routines to launch a new production line. I designed a routine to make sure I didn't miss my 6 am flight. Designer-coaches create plays that are crafted to be successful against a specific opponent's offense or defense. Designer-business owners plan employee activities in a way that eliminates ambiguity.

Think about what you want. Own it. Now, design your actions, responses, and routines to help begin producing the desired result.

Direct

There is nothing worse than having information and not knowing what to do with it.

I remember graduating and having no clue what I wanted to do in my career. I heard about a personality test that would not only tell you what your personality was but would also align it with the jobs that fit your strengths. I was broke but managed to scrounge up the twenty-nine bucks to take the test.

After an hour of answering some very random and seemingly less-than-applicable questions, I finished and downloaded my new profile. Much to my disappointment, the test results produced what was promised. The website populated a list of 20 different general categories of jobs that my personality would fit. There was everything from sales to consulting to professional musician.

I had made a mistake in assuming that the information would give me direction. I had the information, but I didn't know how to translate it into movement.

<u>Accountability should be directing future movement, not just accounting for what has happened in the past.</u>

If what you are measuring is not adjusting future movements, it would be like driving your car looking in the rearview mirror. Your eyes see what is ahead and your hands adjust the wheel to change course, unless you are looking only backward.

Consider this story.

On New Year's Eve in 2012 two men tried to break into a jewelry store in Beaudesert, Australia. After unsuccessfully throwing spark plugs at the glass storefront, the dynamic duo came up with a plan to access the general bathroom attached next door. They took a metal bar and beat through the wall.

Once on the other side, they realized they had miscalculated, and instead of ending up in the bank, they were standing in the local Kentucky Fried Chicken. Undeterred, Dwayne Doolan and Peter Welsh threatened the staff with the metal bar and made off with a whopping $2600 in cash. They were arrested a short time later and charged with robbery.[27]

These two were missing some key pieces of accountability that could have helped give their activities better direction, such as:

1. Crime doesn't pay.
2. Building plans are helpful.
3. KFC is not known for stashing lots of cash.
4. You don't want to go to prison (again).
5. If you work that hard to dig through a wall, you could make more money working a legal, paying job!

I am sure both men had plenty of time to think about these things, after the fact.

Is accountability something you see as looking backward or giving a report on the past? If so, you need to turn about and recognize that accountability helps you define the direction of each step you take into the future.

One way accountability can direct future movement is by giving us feedback that we can use to improve our boundaries.

Think about our friends with the affinity for metal bars and fried chicken. If time in the slammer gives them pause, they may decide to set stronger boundaries to keep from frequenting jail.

<u>Accountability uses knowledge to build better boundaries in order to produce more powerful movement.</u>

Now we understand how to detach from the emotions generated by our activities and gain perspective.

We take time to review the tape!

Without a cloud of emotion, we can intentionally design our activities, responses, and routines in ways that naturally keep us accountable, and move us closer to the desired outcomes.

Finally, feedback or information we generate from our efforts can help strengthen our boundaries and direct our future responses.

If we lay a great foundation and review the tape, what can we expect to produce?

The following chapter unpacks the benefits or fruits that accountability produces when we Elevate Accountability.

Chapter 10

Fruits of Our Labor

It is not difficult to know a thing; what is difficult is to know how to use what you know.

– Han Fei Tzu

_____

Each of the previous Parts of MOVE! has produced something. Clarity showed us how to produce a clear picture of where we want to go. Boundaries gave us tremendous focus by limiting our choices. So, what does accountability produce?

For starters, Elevating Accountability produces **awareness**, a **benchmark** of our progress and the **discipline** we need to continue to move toward our Living Visual.

These valuable gems do not suddenly appear after reading a few chapters on accountability. They are forged over long periods of time, while we exert substantial amounts of energy shaping ourselves and our responses.

When we live in the grind, ask great questions, seek clarity, hammer out boundaries, and strive to challenge ourselves and our assumptions, we emerge holding these **three attributes**.

Self or Situational Awareness

My wife and I had been married for about a year when we were asked to come and speak to a group of teenagers about making smart choices. It was a fun event and we enjoyed encouraging and mentoring young people.

After the event ended, we were walking up to our car, which was parked near a busy highway, and noticed a young girl walking across the highway.

It was twilight and traffic was heavy. Cars raced by at highway speeds, headlights glaring, never hitting the brakes.

I watched as the girl was hit by one of the cars, her body flipping over the top of it. She landed on her back, face up, right in the middle of the street. She was following a girlfriend, who had already crossed the highway. Her friend completely lost it and ran screaming up and down the side of the street.

I can say for certain that when you step out in the middle of a busy highway and stare down oncoming traffic, after seeing a girl be hit by a car, you become very aware of the situation and the environment around you.

I remember my wife bending down and taking the girl's hand, the sounds of the traffic, and the screams of the friend standing on the side of the street. The girl was unconscious and my wife was checking her vitals. I had already called 911 and was trying to describe what had happened and where we were, while directing traffic around the injured girl and my wife.

Eventually, the girl regained consciousness and we were able to help move her to the side of the road.

What struck me hard when everyone was out of the dangerous conditions was the irony of the situation.

My wife and I had just spoken to teenagers about making smart choices. Now, those same teenagers had witnessed an accident that could have been prevented by using awareness of the situation. The girls could have found a safe place to cross the highway. They could have waited until the oncoming traffic had passed. They could have been given a ride to their destination, or home, because it was getting dark. So many simple choices to avoid such a terrible result.

<u>Our awareness of our environment is critical to making good decisions.</u>

> ✴ **When we are accountable, we are constantly looking around us and asking questions.**

What do I see? How do I need to adjust?

We design systems in our life that reinforce our movement. Our friends, family, and community help us see the oncoming cars in our life and they speak truth to us to keep us from getting hurt.

When accountability is part of our frame of mind, it makes us better. We become more aware of the world around us and can detach from the emotions of the situation and evaluate each moment on its own merits.

If we fail in this awareness, then we let an idea sweep us away and our emotions blind us to the oncoming traffic. We are not accountable, and instead of getting better and moving closer to our goals, desires, and ambitions, we move farther away.

Own it. Be accountable. Design accountability structures in your daily life, in your business and in your relationships to keep them on track and focused.

Measurable goals

Remember the story about the Milliken Magnolia plant? The difference between employees in a productive and accountable environment and a nonproductive and chaotic environment is found by answering one question: *How do you know when you've had a good day?*

The productive employees know exactly how to respond.

Why? Because the leadership of the company had clearly stated what accomplishment that person was responsible for AND how to measure their progress.

171

Conversely, when leadership doesn't set clear expectations and have never clearly communicated to all employees what and how they can measure success, those employees will simply create their own, poorly directed responses.

Writing down goals is a tremendous step in accountability.

Whether in business or our personal lives, it has long been proven that we are more likely to accomplish something if we have written it down. We own it when we write it. It becomes more physical and less of just an idea. Writing down goals is critical, but isn't enough. Take the next logical step.

Ask yourself: how am I going to be accountable to respond in ways that make this become my reality? How will I know if I am moving closer to it or farther away?

If you can answer these two questions, you have a goal that is measurable.

When we write down a goal, we automatically give ourselves a benchmark. A goal can be a standard. We can design our routines in ways that help produce that standard. Then, we can measure our progress toward it.

Discipline

When I started college, I was given a course book that listed all the classes and when I would take them. My entire four years of school was summed up in just a few pages. I remember being alone in my room at the time and having a total freshman freak-out moment. Some of the course descriptions were completely foreign to me, and I thought, "If I can't even understand the course description, how the heck am I going to pass the class?"

Then for half an hour, I played mental images of me telling my parents I flunked out.

After a while, a small still voice said, "Snap out of it, man!" and I realized that it was not my job to know everything in the course book the first day of my freshmen year.

Nope, my job was work on what I had to do that day. That was it. Just focus on the task at hand, and then move to the next one.

> If we hold ourselves accountable to move a little each day, we become accustomed to small wins and train our brains to reach for and gather even more.

Intentional discipline teaches our mind that the impossible is possible, one step at a time. Seeing what needs to be done and following through is living with discipline.

When the information we collect on our activities and responses drive our behavior, it produces healthy routines, instead of agonizing decisions. We can learn to break free of reacting to every issue and start realizing the power of intentional response.

When we have a treasure trove of daily accomplishments we can see in our wake, it encourages our heart and mind to undertake the whole challenge ahead. We have done the little things we said we would. We take on the big thing and say we will. Our mind and body follow along because of what we have experienced in the past.

~~~

Men talk about having no future and no hope before becoming a part of Homes of Hope. They had nothing. No money. No car. No job. No future.

And then it is so encouraging to hear them tell about how Homes of Hope met them where they were and, without judgment, started building them back up.

They gave them a place to live but expected them to keep it clean. They gave them a job but expected them to show up and work hard. They helped them develop a marketable skill and taught them how to manage their money.

And when the men leave the program, their confidence is obvious. They are joyful. They feel empowered to create a bright future. They speak with conviction because they have come from rock bottom, one step at a time. They have learned discipline and hard work, and they believe it will lead them to a brighter future.

When you Elevate Accountability and own your responses, you gain discipline, because you have identified what you want to create and actively measure how your responses move you toward it.

Pretty soon, you turn around and don't recognize the person looking back at you from the mirror.

Accountability over time, changes you into a better you.

Tips on Becoming More Accountable

<u>Start small</u> – If you can be responsible and accountable for small things, it will make it easier to be accountable for big things. Even if it's just not automatically salting your food or not checking social media until lunch. Train your brain.

One of our daughters has a tough time controlling her temper. When she was just two years old, she once started crying and couldn't stop. She went from crying to total meltdown.

We taught her to put her hands together when she started to cry. Not much, but we thought if a two-year-old can get their hands together while crying, that little act of discipline can help them control their emotions.

The results were amazing.

At first, she struggled and even rejected the notion. However, over time, if she could get her hands together, then she would stop crying and avoid a tantrum.

She realized at this very young age that she was in control of her emotions. That control helped her to respond instead of reacting, and it all began with something as small as putting her hands together.

Don't wait – We discussed that accountability flows out of clarity and we use accountability to design the work. So, don't wait until after you are executing to figure out how to account for it. Start now in understanding how you are going to measure and account for your progress.

Once the Wild Turkey bourbon starts blazing and running down the hill, it's too late to check if there is a fire hydrant.

Pillar III Review

In Chapter 8, we began by asking a very simple question: *how do you know what you know?*

One of the most important ways we Elevate Accountability is by tying our intentional actions, responses, and routines to a **standard**. The standard comes out of clarity and is within our boundaries. When we generate clarity and use it to set standards in our lives we "know what we know."

Chapter 9, Building a Foundation, showed us how to develop measurements that **reinforced** the types of responses necessary for success.

One of the most important aspects of owning our path forward is taking time to make sure our actions, responses, and routines are **meaningful**. Will they produce what we want to produce?

Accountability means we pay attention to all the details, even small ones that could affect the path forward.

In Chapter 10, we discovered another great accountability question: *how do you know you have had a good day?*

When we are in the moment, it's difficult to be aware of how we are doing, as relates to our goal. We are in the middle of daily battles and the grind of producing our future.

However, we can step back and **detach** from the emotion involved in execution to regain perspective.

We also must be able to pro-actively **design** routine activities and responses that increase the likelihood that we will achieve our intentions. If we detach from emotion and design activities thoughtfully, they produce valuable information.

However, that information is only **valuable** if we use it to direct future movements.

Finally, when we Elevate Accountability, we reap several rewards.

We have more **awareness** of ourselves and the situation. We can **measure** our progress toward realistic **goals** and develop the **discipline** necessary to achieve them.

All the pieces are in place: Clarity, Boundaries, Accountability. Time to execute!

Pillar IV
Intentionally Execute

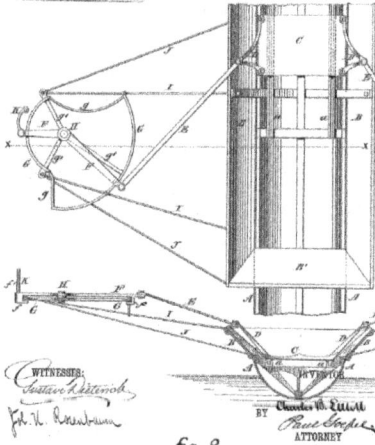

fig. 8

"When all is said and done, more is said than done."

– Lou Holtz

"To be is to do."

– Socrates

It was a party. My wife's sister and brother-in-law had purchased a home nearby and we wanted to have them over for lunch to welcome them to the neighborhood.

As we finished setting the table and preparing the meal, we were all talking together in the kitchen and dining room. My brother-in-law and I were standing at a dining room window, watching a summer storm raging outside. It was raining sheets of water and thunder was shaking the house.

BOOM! Suddenly, a bolt of lightning shot from the sky and hit a tree about 50 yards in front of the window.

You can imagine the scene that followed; kids are crying and yelling, running through the house, my wife and her sister hurrying in from the kitchen, asking if our house had been struck. I assured them it hadn't been hit and pointed to the row of beautiful white pines on the other side of our driveway.

"Do you see that tree on the end of the row? The bolt hit the tree about 10 feet up the trunk," I said. Everyone was looking out the window. Sure enough, about 10 feet up on the back of the tree we saw a small flame.

My wife shrieked, "It's on fire!" No problem, I thought, the rain was still coming down in buckets and would surely put out any small fire that the lightning had produced.

But . . . it didn't.

As we stood and watched, that small flicker grew and grew. From about the size of a golf ball to the size of a baseball. Then, the fire grew to the size of a basketball and started climbing up the tree.

One thing is for sure. I could see what was about to happen. That row of huge, beautiful, white pine trees ran along the driveway and hung right over our garage. Next stop, the house.

As the fire grew, I knew I had two choices, call 911 and hope that the fire department could make it before the row of pines burned up like a torch or put out the fire before it got out of control. Anyone who has seen a Christmas tree catch on fire knows what was about to happen.

So, I took off.

In just a few seconds I grabbed the largest fire extinguisher we had in the house and ran out the front door barefoot, charging across the yard like a knight into battle.

About halfway across the yard, a second BOOM sounded, and an instant later, I realized the risk of my situation. I was standing on a hill, beside a tree, in the middle of a terrible lightning storm, holding a large metal container – in my bare feet! I almost turned around, but I saw molten sap dripping out the back of the tree and catching the ground on fire.

Luckily, I was able to reach the tree without getting struck by lightning. My large fire extinguisher had been difficult to carry and was dusty from sitting in the back of the pantry, but it worked perfectly. In a matter of seconds, the fire was out and I was racing back to take cover on the porch.

I felt so alive. I was totally out of breath, soaking wet, had almost been struck by lightning – and I felt AMAZING!

And why?

Because I chose to move.

No matter how many times you practice on the ground, you don't feel the rush until you jump out of the plane.

It is the movement that makes us feel alive. **When we choose to Intentionally Execute it energizes us.**

We have arrived in the final part of the book and no matter how much clarity you have or how good your boundaries are or that you have tremendous accountability, if you don't MOVE! it doesn't matter.

As Socrates so eloquently stated, "To be is to DO." So, stop waiting and start doing. If you don't move now, all the work and thought you have put in up to this point is for nothing.

The idea of someone rowing is the perfect picture to represent Pillar IV: Intentionally Execute. We have mapped out our direction (Clarity), built the boat that will take us where we want to go (Boundaries), we know our stroke count and can hear the coxswains adjustments (Accountability) and now it is time to take hold of the oars and pull.

Execution in our lives is like rowing, we must keep pulling. Whether things are falling into place or falling apart, we must keep moving.

Movement gives us consistency through the ups and downs of life. We can execute regardless of the state of our circumstances.

Although we may face uncertainty, we can certainly MOVE!

In Pillar IV, we are going to discover the *Five Paths* and learn the *Movement Mindset*.

We will conclude Pillar IV with the chapter, Turning the Flywheel, which gives some practical wisdom that's helpful to remember while we MOVE!

Throughout the final chapters, we will explore how to translate Seek Clarity, Develop Boundaries, and Elevate Accountability into action – beginning the move from where we are, to where we want to be.

Chapter 11

Finding the Five Paths

There are not more than five musical notes, yet the combinations of these five give rise to more melodies than can ever be heard.

There are not more than five primary colors, yet in combination they produce more hues than can ever been seen.

There are not more than five cardinal tastes, yet combinations of them yield more flavors than can ever be tasted.

– Sun Tzu, The Art of War

The Greek word for happiness or welfare is "Eudaimonia." Aristotle and Plato agreed that the main goal of our lives was to seek and discover how to live well.

However, Aristotle asserted that there was great disagreement on what type of living could be counted as living well and spent significant time exploring how people find happiness or well-being.

In *Nicomachean Ethics*, his major work on ethics, Aristotle writes that Eudaimonia involves activity in harmony with reason, and believed that the highest use and ideal work for humans incorporated a perfect exercise of reason.

Shawn Achor, Harvard researcher and writer, sums up Aristotle by defining happiness as "the joy you feel moving toward your potential".[28]

To Aristotle, reason does not end in thought alone, but in action. So, he deduced that we are happiest when we develop our ability to <u>act on our reason</u>. We create meaningful movement in our life at that very moment!

> ✸ *Knowing what to do and performing it with excellence increases our happiness.*

Aristotle and Socrates argued that virtue and character are part of reason, so exercising character enables a person to exercise his reason.

This means our character or inner self is an important factor in reason. Other factors included in reason would be competency and mindset.

Modern writers, like David Brooks, a columnist for the New York Times and contributor to PBS NewsHour and Meet the Press, echoes Aristotle in his book, *The Road to Character*.

Brooks discusses the idea of a higher- and a lower-self. He names the lower-self, Adam I. This lower-self exhibits tendencies we all have, such as self-centeredness, pride, jealousy, misguided ambition, greed and a multitude of other perverse natures.

Regardless of our piety, background, family, social status or race, we all share the common "bugs in our nature"[29] – lower order desires that drive our lives but deliver little satisfaction.

There is also a higher-self Brooks calls Adam II. This higher-self has qualities like humility, gratitude, and companionship. These examples of higher qualities are desirable and provide deep satisfaction when lived out. Aristotle and Socrates' "virtue" would be related to a person's ability to intentionally reason higher-self thinking to produce long-term well-being. Movement that produces happiness is rooted in the higher-self.

In Pillar I: Seek Clarity, we covered how to build a clear picture of what we want to move toward. The Living Visual guides boundaries we set and results we hold ourselves accountable to achieve. Our clarity and subsequent movement may be around a relationship, a business, a job, kids, finances, or even a state of being.

As we begin to execute and move toward our Living Visual, we face seemingly infinite paths to move along.

However, just like the quote at the beginning of this chapter about the five primary colors being the basis for all colors, there are **Five Paths** where we can exert energy to create the movement necessary to close gaps in our lives.

The Five Paths are fundamental approaches; and just like blending primary colors to create an entire palette, the paths may overlap or crisscross, so we may often travel down more than one at the same time.

The Five Paths are filled with activities from our higher-self, not simple responses to stimuli.

When your doctor hits your knee with that little hammer and your leg jumps, the movement is simply a response to the physical stimuli. We don't intentionally think about responding, it just happens. No wrestling with ideas or ideals. No morals. No nothing, just a rubber hammer and a knee-jerk.

In contrast, when we move down one or more of the Five Paths and operate within our higher-order selves, we begin with an *intention*.

Why does an artist paint? Why does a carpenter build? There is something in them that drives them to create.

When we operate and move in higher-self activities, we experience satisfaction and meaning in our work and lives.

If we find happiness and produce meaningful work, it is by following at least one or more of the **Five Paths**:

fig. 9
THE FIVE PATHS

When we create movement, we travel down at least one or more of these Five Paths. Think of them as the options you have at your disposal when you are ready to take on the world.

> At our best higher-selves, we want to create, order, restore, renew, and grow – all while using our unique gifts to serve others for the greater good.

In Pillar I: Seek Clarity, we covered the idea of intimately understanding what we want to achieve. When we solve problems or overcome challenges in our lives, we travel down one of the Five Paths, creating movement from an internal strength of character and deep alignment with our purpose. The journey is what produces deep satisfaction and happiness. *We attain satisfaction when we connect our actions with something greater than ourselves.*

If we realize that our movement is helping us reach our potential, we can find greater meaning in our activities.

How much satisfaction do you feel when you **create order** out of chaos? It could be as simple as organizing your closet. Doesn't it make you feel good when you **restore** something? Maybe an old piece of furniture or a prior friendship? Either way, it makes you feel great!

The Five Paths give us an idea of directional movement in our lives and a sense that our movement is meaningful, <u>because they are hardwired into our being.</u>

Exploring the Five Paths

Each of the Five Paths are unique in how they help us <u>close the gaps between where we are and where we want to be.</u> They always exist as options in our journey and traveling down one does not mean the others are unavailable to us. Sometimes they cross and overlap, and just as we sometimes need to adjust our boundaries to accommodate changing situations or circumstances, we may need to utilize more than one of the Five Paths.

Let's look at each path in more detail.

To Create

One of the most powerful and rewarding of the paths we choose is to create. We create when we bring ideas, products, relationships, and people into being. Before we create, there may only be a thought. Then, we make the thought a reality. Artists, entrepreneurs, builders, and skilled craftsmen are just some trades who create.

We also create new relationships, families, and, yes, babies.

Creating often ends in a natural high. We can see the product of our hard work and the contribution we have given to the world.

Think about your life. Do you have a burning desire to create something new? It could be anything – a new product, clothing design, tech-device, knowledge, relationship or song.

Let's look at Henry Ford, a man who understood the necessity of creation.

In 1913, he desired to close the gap between the general public and car ownership. He determined a way to mass-produce automobiles and created the moving assembly line. It was a brilliant idea that ultimately lowered the cost of manufacturing so much that the 'average Joe' could afford the new luxury of an automobile.

His new creation doubled production without increasing his workforce. Sounds great, except that a new problem, tied to implementing his idea emerged.

Ford had paid the going wage rate, but the new assembly line configuration required each worker to be highly specialized and proficient at a repetitive task. Workers began leaving in droves, which made the turnover rate skyrocket and forced Ford to keep thousands of potential employees on call for the daily workforce shortages.[30]

Facing this obstacle, after creating such innovation, how did Henry Ford create movement in his company?

He did something radical.

On January 5, 1914, Henry Ford made a jaw-dropping announcement: he would be doubling factory worker's average daily wage; cutting the work-day from 9 to 8 hours; and adding a third shift.

Ford adjusted his Living Visual and created new elements that would allow for a stable workforce, and the fullest utilization of his creation, the moving assembly line.

By the following day, an army of job seekers that would eventually number 12,000 appeared at the plant gates. Fights broke out and the police had to be called to keep the peace. Within a week, Ford received 14,000 more applications by mail. Within one week, Ford went from having 1,400 employees not showing up for work to having 26,000 people begging to work for him. What happened next turned out to be remarkable.

The turnover rate fell from 370% to 16%. Productivity was up 40% and the replacement workers would fall from 53,000 to 2,000. Between 1914 and 1916, Ford's profits doubled from $30 million to $60 million.

Henry Ford created radically new conditions for his workers that allowed him to close the gap of where he wanted to be: producing cars affordable for the general public.

Creating is awesome!

To Restore

When we restore, our goal is to bring something back to its original glory or condition; to bring back whatever has been lost, taken or broken; to add energy to a person, relationship, or thing to make it whole.

A good friend of ours has Type II Diabetes. She realized that this disease could bring about a decline in her health. So, she made up her mind to do whatever was necessary to change the trajectory of her health, with her ultimate goal being to get off insulin completely. She found a specialist in the field, who believed the right diet would allow her insulin to be dramatically reduced, or even eliminated. The diet was brutally strict and very different from her diet for decades; however, she was determined, and her transformation has been dramatic and amazing!

She chose to walk down the path of *restoration*. She is restoring her health to what it was years earlier. At the age of 72, her bloodwork results now are similar to results in her 40s!

We are proud of her for making the decision to move. She feels great and looks like a new person. As a bonus, she is almost completely off insulin shots. She was able to accomplish great movement in her life over the age of 70 by walking down the path of restoration.

To Renew

People who lived through the Great Depression and World War II were very skilled at the art and science of renewal. To **renew** is similar to restore, but where something has been used, broken, or lost, instead of bringing back its original glory, we transform it into something new.

When I was 8 years old, while I was playing out in the yard, my grandfather pulled into the driveway. As he got out of his car, I could tell he was excited. He had found (or made) a toy for my brothers and me.

I was pumped! New toys, hurray!

He reached into his car and pulled out a metal wire about 3 feet long, with a U-shaped bend in one end and a wooden handle on the other. Then, he pulled out a metal ring that was a little smaller in diameter than a basketball.

He looked at me, smiled, and said, "Here you go."

I asked him what it was. I had no idea.

He explained that when he was a kid, they had wagons on the farm. When a wagon wheel broke and was no longer able to be repaired, the kids would pop the ring off the hub of the wooden wheel, bend some wire and turn it into a toy. He had found or bought a ring from an old wagon wheel and made a toy for us.

"What do I do with it?" I was still trying to figure out how you play with a metal ring and a wire. He told me to roll the metal ring, and then use the U-shape end of the wire to push it forward.

"If you practice, you can keep the ring balanced and rolling without letting it fall over." So, I rolled the ring and took off down the driveway chasing it with my U-shaped metal wire.

So, even an old wagon wheel can be renewed. It was no longer a wagon wheel, and instead was a brand "new" toy. It was also great exercise!

To Order

To **order** is to bring structure and thoughtfulness into chaos and disarray. When we order, we exert energy over something we control, so we can order its design and make it perform in a consistent and meaningful way.

One of my favorite news topics is new gene therapies and the coming explosion of new treatments in the field of medicine. It seems that humanity may be getting close to curing some diseases that, until now, would be impossible to treat or even cure.

On Nov. 13 of 2017 in California, 44-year-old Brian Madeux was the first person to be treated using a new gene therapy technique.[31]

Through an IV, Brian received billions of copies of a corrective gene, and a genetic tool to cut his DNA in a precise spot. His birth DNA was actually altered.

It was similar to the old Raquel Welch movie, where scientists and surgeons were shrunk and sent in a tiny submarine through the human body. This new procedure allowed the new gene to be placed in exactly the right location.

It is amazing to me we live in a time when this is possible. However, when you hear doctors talk about the procedure, it sounds like my 4-year-old telling me how she put her Minnie Mouse puzzle together:

"We cut your DNA, open it up, insert a gene, stitch it back up. Invisible mending," said Dr. Sandy Macrae, president of Sangamo Therapeutics, the California company testing this for two metabolic diseases and hemophilia. "It becomes part of your DNA and is there for the rest of your life."

No big deal, right? A snip here and a snip there of your DNA, and then replace it with a few new stitches, altering the way you experience reality for the rest of your life.

To me that is mindboggling **order**. *We take something that needs deliberate attention and change it in a way that more consistently produces the results we desire.*

Order up!

To Grow

When we think about growing, we may think about trees getting taller or a kid's voice cracking during puberty.

That *is* growth, but as we look at growth relating to movement or relating to the Five Paths, I want to offer a different perspective.

Growth in our context means a *change in response*.

> **You grow as a person when you are faced with a recurring situation but choose a new response that produces a better result.**

Have you seen movies that dramatize our lives by painting the picture that some environments and people never change?

Think about the old TV show, "Cheers" – *"Where everybody knows your name!"*

The premise of this sitcom was that most of the main characters have been in the bar forever. Everything outside the bar gives them plenty to talk about, but that core environment never changes. The characters all embody certain personalities and they rarely change. No surprises.

We feel good when we feel like we are in control. It's the warm safety blanket in our mind. If we can't control everything, we relate to our Cheers bar or even try to create the atmosphere and environment in our own lives. Consistency, control, and perfect relationships. What's not to like?!

Unfortunately, the idea that our lives remain still, fixed or static is a myth and not a true option.

On the opposite end of the spectrum, we see the harm that people experience when they feel like they have lost all control. Traumatic experiences, like the death of a spouse or a natural disaster, can cause many people to shut down. It can cause some people to develop destructive or addictive coping habits. Life with no control or consistency is headed for destruction.

We need some consistency in our lives, some foundation to give us stability and peace of mind.

Your life and the world around it is in motion. There are opportunities that fall into your lap. There are disasters knocking on your door. There are people you trust deeply who break that trust. There are people who carry you when you fail.

A small boy was born in the mid-1600's. His father had died three months before he was born, leaving his mother widowed. To make matters worse, he was born prematurely and was so small his mother said that he could fit inside a "quart mug."

When he was only three years old, his mother remarried and left him in the care of his grandmother.

What a tragic start in life! There were tremendous forces being pushed onto the boy, and he had no control over each of those hardships.

Maybe it was those early years that formed Isaac Newton into a man who would become one of the most influential scientists in history, developing calculus, the laws of motion and gravitation, and a theory of color.

Students today learn Newton's three laws of motion in physics. The third law is:

"For every action, there is an equal and opposite reaction."

As external and internal forces play out in our lives, some bring order and direction, while others bring chaos and uncertainty. Many times, we have no control over the forces that create positive or negative situations. **However, we can control our response to those situations.**

Decisions have momentum. One leads to another, leading to another, and yet another.

Individuals who are successful in life (not just rich and famous) are individuals who realize exactly what they can and cannot control.

We have no control over our past experiences. They have shaped who we are today, but as my grandmother used to say, "There's no use crying over spilled milk!"

We also have very little control over forces, tragedies, and circumstances that are levied against us. Natural disasters, war, crime, death, and so many other forces are completely out of our control.

However, by taking control of our response or changing our response, we help produce new experiences. Who do you want to be in 10 years? How you grow all depends on how you respond each day.

> *Movement is taking small steps towards a future self or future state you desire.*

One statistic that has always fascinated me is the number of professional football players who make millions of dollars but declare bankruptcy within two years of leaving the NFL.

In 2009, Sports Illustrated ran an article titled, *Why (and how) Players Go Broke*. According to the article, 78% of all NFL players will be bankrupt or broke within two years after leaving the league.[32]

The article explained that one of the major reasons that NFL players go broke so fast is that, after leaving the league, their annual paycheck goes down dramatically, but their lifestyle expenses remain the same.

Let's look at how a change in our response not only shows growth but creates a different future. Look at the timeline and decisions below:

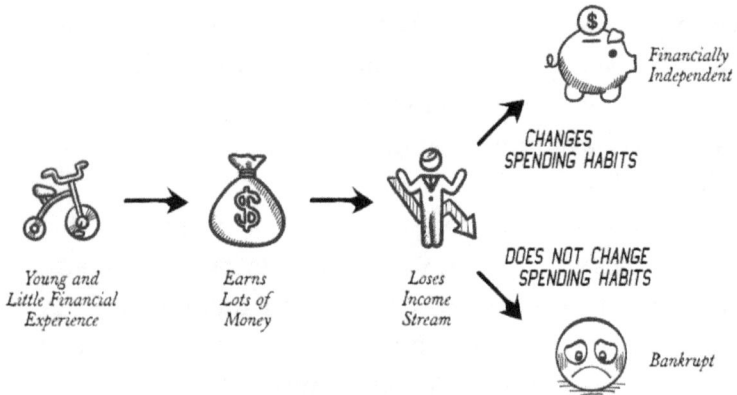

fig. 10
RESPONSIBILITY SHAPES REALITY

In one scenario the individual does not change their response to how they manage and spend money, and they go bankrupt.

In the other scenario, the person *grows*, changes their response to spending in accordance with their new income, and remains financially independent.

Growth occurs when we change ourselves to meet the challenges around us.

We may think if we want a future self that is generous, we need millions of dollars to create that generosity. Winning the lottery then becomes a destination, and generosity the result.

However, **the truth is**: if we desire generosity, life will require sacrifice, so we can be generous. If we desire loyalty, life will test our commitment, so that we can prove we are loyal. If we desire honesty, life will present unethical opportunities, so we can act in a higher, moral manner. We must be careful to see those challenges as growth opportunities, rather than negative events.

We grow when we change our responses to meet the curveballs life throws our way.

Chapter 12

The Movement Mindset

We are always getting ready to live, but never living.
                                    – Ralph Waldo Emmerson

———————————

Movement takes energy, determination and resolve. The most important thing to remember as we create movement in our life is being mindful of our **mindset**.

In this chapter, we will unpack six critical *Movement Mindsets* that are necessary to maintain positive momentum in life and our work.

1. Prepare for Opportunity
2. Slow is Smooth; Smooth is Fast
3. Serve the Work
4. Value Flexibility
5. Pursue Mastery Versus Success
6. Embrace Suffering

The Movement Mindsets are valuable keys to **successful execution** and are principle-driven.

Mindset #1 – Prepare for Opportunity

We have moved our fire extinguishers through two different states and at least three houses over the years. They were dusty and in the back of the pantry the day lightning struck our pine tree, but they became indispensable. When we took the actions to stock those red fire extinguishers, we were creating movement toward protecting our home against fire.

Preparation is not something you do _before_ you move — preparation IS movement.

We don't feel preparation. No one is going to tackle you in a hardware store and beg you to buy a fire extinguisher. When you get to work, you won't look around and see co-workers walking around with the latest and greatest fire extinguisher, pressuring you into buying one (unless you work at the fire department). But when you need it, you need it.

Preparation is pro-active.

When you prepare, you are responding to an event before the event takes place. You are pro-active in responding to create a future that you desire.

I prefer my house not burn down, so I keep fire extinguishers close by.

Preparation shows that we take opportunity seriously.

When my wife and I were newlyweds, we were completely broke. It didn't stop us from going to see a financial planner though, and he gave me some of the best financial advice I have ever received. I asked him about trying to flip houses with no money down, and about three other get-rich-quick ideas. He told me not to be impatient, but to prepare for opportunity. Sure, the mega-mansion in bankruptcy is for sale, but if you can't afford it, it's not a real opportunity for you.

His advice not only helped me set great financial boundaries, but it offered great clarity about how we should approach our finances.

Dabo Swinney and the Clemson Tigers won the National College Football Championship in January of 2017. The game was a grudge match against the powerhouse Alabama's Crimson Tide, and a rematch from the National Championship a year before.

But, let's back up to the beginning of the 2015 season, on a hot summer day in August at a team meeting, long before Alabama and Clemson faced in their first National Championship matchup.

The team had taken a retreat offsite, and at the end of the gathering, Dabo said he had a special announcement. He then awarded scholarships to junior punter, Andy Teasdall and redshirt freshman wide receiver, Hunter Renfrow.

The following is an excerpt from the speech he gave as he handed out the awards:

> "... We love all you guys, and it's always a blessing when I get a chance to reward a guy. This guy right here just came out to a spring tryout. Yeah, he might have a chance. All he did was come out and work and work and work and prepare. He was preparing for an opportunity he didn't know he'd ever get.
>
> Isn't that one of the lessons we talk about?
>
> <u>Prepare for your opportunity, even if it never comes.</u> Better to be prepared without an opportunity than to not be prepared with one. What a great lesson . . ."[33]

Fast forward through two seasons to the 2017 National Championship. The game is on the line. There is time for one more play. The star quarterback Deshaun Watson drops back to pass. Who does he throw it to? A former walk-on, Hunter Renfrow.

Two years after being awarded a walk-on scholarship for his hard work, Renfrow caught the game-winning pass in the end zone to clinch the National Championship. No one could have written a better storybook ending.

We choose how we respond to life and our circumstances every day. We need to <u>choose to prepare for opportunity,</u> so when it arrives we can embrace it and maximize the movement it creates.

What do you know you should be doing right now to prepare for opportunity?

Mindset #2 – Slow is Smooth; Smooth is Fast

If you have ever taken a trip to a shooting range, had a lesson in target practice, or know someone in the military, you have probably heard the saying, "Slow is smooth and smooth is fast."

It sounds strange at first. It seems contradictory, but the saying sums up a great principle of how we move and improve.

When we learn new things through experience, especially a skill like shooting a gun or playing a musical instrument, it takes deliberate practice. You don't start shooting a gun like Wild Bill or playing an instrument like Yo-Yo Ma the first day. You can't rush it. You must start training your fingers, arms, legs, eyes, and mind to respond in a certain way. Repetition, over time, trains your mind and body.

At the beginning of target practice, a student's goal is not to shoot fast, but to hit the target.

To do so, we must draw with a smooth action, level the gun, aim, and fire. As your body gets used to the motion, feel, and rhythm of shooting at a target, you can gradually increase the speed, until the point where you begin to lose "smoothness." When your technique becomes choppy, you will lose accuracy or speed.

Deliberate practice is performing the activity correctly on the transition point where achieving smooth action is difficult. You keep pushing the line of where you can perform the action with perfection and where you lose control. Gradually, you get better, smoother, faster.

The masters of any skill have put in thousands of hours of deliberate practice to make the task they perform look effortless. Think of a musician playing Bach or Mozart or even a Jimmy Hendrix riff.

When it's time to move, remember: Slow is smooth, smooth is fast.

When we move, it can be messy.

Sometimes we move into uncharted territory, so we need to move slowly until we figure out what works. Once we've done that, we can move a little faster, and then a little faster.

The Movement Mindset is not a sprint, but a marathon.

There should be no expectation of speed at first, but a concentration on how well we can correctly execute our task at hand. We may not have perfected our execution yet, but soon it will be smooth enough to increase our speed. Speed comes with experience and expertise. *Patience is a virtue, take the long view when you move.*

Mindset #3 – Serve the Work (not the community)

Serve your work. Be great at doing great things, regardless of what the community thinks – and by community, I mean the world.

Serving the work may sound confusing, when we spent so much time developing a community and listening to their feedback in order to Seek Clarity. Our work is how we serve others right? Absolutely. Our communities help us construct our clarity and keep us on the right track, right? Correct!

So, how do we serve the work but live in community?

Listen to how Dorothy Sayers answers the question. She was a famous British mystery writer in the twentieth century and was also one of the first women awarded a degree from Oxford University. Dorothy wrote many plays and crime mysteries, but she also wrote about the importance of work.

In her essay titled, "Why Work?" she considers many ideas, one of which centers around how we should serve our work before trying to serve the community at large. Here is Dorothy's advice:

There is, in fact, a paradox about working to serve the community, and it is this: that to aim directly at serving the community is to falsify the work; the only way to serve the community is to forget the community and serve the work. There are three very good reasons for this: The first is that you cannot do good work if you take your mind off the work to see how the community is taking it – any more than you can make a good drive from the tee if you take your eye off the ball. "Blessed are the single-hearted: (for that is the real meaning of the word we translate "the pure in heart"). If your heart is not wholly in the work, the work will not be good – and work that is not good serves neither God nor the community; it only serves mammon.

The second reason is that the moment you think of serving other people, you begin to have a notion that other people owe you something for your pains; you begin to think that you have a claim on the community. You will begin to bargain for reward, to angle for applause, and to harbor a grievance if you are not appreciated. But if your mind is set upon serving the work, then you know you have nothing to look for; the only reward the work can give you is the satisfaction of beholding its perfection. The work takes all and gives nothing but itself; and to serve the work is a labor of pure love.

And thirdly, if you set out to serve the community, you will probably end by merely fulfilling a public demand – and you may not even do that. A public demand is a changeable thing . . . The danger of "serving the community" is that one is part of the community, and that in serving it one may only be serving a kind of communal egotism. The only true way of serving the community is to be truly in sympathy with the community, to be oneself part of the community and then to serve the work without giving the community another thought. Then the work will endure, because it will be true to itself. It is the work that serves the community; the business of the worker is to serve the work.[34]

Dorothy Sayer said a lot about serving the work, but her points can be reduced to a few simple ideas.

Her first point revolves around the *focus* required to produce great work. If we are executing and exerting great energy to produce valuable work, we must maintain tremendous focus to make sure the work we produce is excellent. Sometimes people and their opinions can be a distraction.

Focus is what we learned how to develop in Pillar II: Develop Boundaries.

The second idea is concerned with the *intention* of the person working. If we shift our intention toward pleasing others more than producing quality work, our motives and intentions become more political. We give other people control on how the work is done, rather than our internal desire for excellence.

In Pillar I: Seek Clarity, we discovered the importance of gaining clarity on exactly what we want. Our intentions spring out of knowing what we want and moving toward it.

Her final argument on why we should serve the work is based on maintaining a pure *motivation*. Some work should be completed because of "its own integrity." Dorothy is not suggesting we shouldn't want people to pay us for our work; rather, she is suggesting that, on the whole, money should matter less to us than the quality of what we produce.

> **Our work and the integrity of our work reflects the integrity of who we are as individuals.**

For example, in my Nashville example, it would be easy to be motivated to change careers to become famous. Dorothy would say I should move because I want to be a great songwriter and write great songs regardless of any fame or acclaim.

We are part of a larger community. Our work serves the community, and we serve the work.

What Dorothy is <u>not</u> saying is that we should close our ears and our minds and live on an island while we work.

On the contrary, she is suggesting that we do whatever it takes to create, order, renew, restore, and grow in our work. We focus all our resources and efforts to that end. We take in any, and all, helpful information if it helps us better our craft. And most importantly, we look at the results of our work to make sure we are serving it well.

If we truly want to serve our communities, family and the world in general, we must start by serving the work we do. We must be motivated by the value of the work itself, not what the work will produce in superfluous benefits.

Don't miss an opportunity to be great in your work. If you are going to start a business, focus on building a great one. If you are going to get married, don't long to be in other marriages, serve the work and create an amazing marriage. If you move toward having kids, focus on the work of raising children to have skills and talents that they can give back to the world.

Mindset #4 – Value Flexibility

Earlier in the book we discussed the difference between boundaries and barriers. We understood that boundaries help us focus our efforts to produce success, while barriers are those obstacles that stand in the way of our success.

Overcoming barriers requires resiliency, and resiliency requires flexibility. Flexibility is the ability to bend but not break when facing an obstacle or barrier. Being flexible increases our resiliency because it allows us to take hits or setbacks without sustaining catastrophic failure.

During the American Revolutionary War, General Francis Marion became an expert at being flexible.

After sustaining losses against a British force far superior in numbers and weapons, Francis Marion, a.k.a. The Swamp Fox, designed a strategy that allowed him and his fighters to be more flexible. He stashed supplies at multiple sights, so that if the enemy attacked one of the sites, he would not lose all his supplies. He also ordered his troops to carry light supplies and ammunition, so they could move faster. Most of his army was on horseback so they could move cross-country faster than the enemy. He even used a unique breed of horses, the Carolina Marsh Tacky, because they could pass through the swamps easier than larger horses. The reins of the horses bridles were not tied and all his men's horses were trained to follow their master so they could be mounted in a moment.[35]

When in battle, the Swamp Fox's plans and orders were always simple, so they could be quickly communicated and understood. He rarely fought the larger opponent head-on, and instead utilized surprise attacks and guerrilla warfare tactics – and it worked.

In the battle at Black Mingo, General Marion's troops crossed over a wooden bridge in the middle of the night. To ensure stealth, he ordered his men to lay blankets down along the bridge to dampen the sound.[36]

The Swamp Fox adjusted to the enemy quickly, was more mobile, and not constrained to a fort or single supply line. It was his flexibility that gave his army the ability to succeed against a superior opponent.

When we face difficult problems, barriers, and obstacles in our life, we must remember that the most direct path may not always be open.

So — Don't give up! Find another way. Use your noodle and be creative. Humans have a dramatic capacity for creativity that helps enhance our flexibility.

When approaching a problem or an obstacle, there may be many potential solutions that help us achieve victory. Remember, the barrier that blocks us can become the way to move – look beyond the straight path.

Mindset #5 – Success vs. Mastery

What is the difference between success and mastery?

Success is accomplishing what we set out to do. It may be financial, social, spiritual, political, or personal in nature.

However, success is difficult because if we move toward success, we may achieve it. If we achieve it, we will be happy, but that happiness is unsustainable.

Where do you go from the top? The only road is downhill.

Many of us may dream of winning the NBA championship when we are 23. Or maybe we dream of making a hit album that tops the music charts when we are 25. Forget the work of music and sports, some of us would just prefer to win the Powerball Lottery and walk away with several hundred million dollars! Our culture views each of these moments as examples of extreme success.

The realities of extreme success can be difficult to navigate.

If you just won the gold at the Olympics, almost before you could make it to the locker room a reporter would be asking you if you were planning to compete again in four years.

It would be easy for your mind to start wondering if you could compete and train that hard for that long.

Sometimes you may ask yourself, "What is next?" or "What am I supposed to do now?" Someone who achieves a very high level of success could easily feel the burden of having to repeat the success or feeling like a failure.

As soon as you win a gold medal at the Olympics, you make it on the gold medal winners list. Before winning, you only wanted just to win one. After winning, you see everyone on the list above your name who have won many gold medals. The temptation may be asking, "Why not me?" Success can be dangerous when it presents additional complications to our lives.

It could be easy to dismiss the illustration about extreme success by arguing that it is unlikely to happen to us. But the problem is, challenges arising from success come from all success, not just the extreme version. Managing success is easier when we keep it in its proper place. Success is achieved, but is not the end.

Healthy success is just part of the journey. Just like failure. Neither failure nor success are destinations but are more like milestones that mark the path through our lives.

You don't want to miss the importance of this paradox.

Success is not bad or good; and it is my hope that anyone who reads and applies the principles in this book would become more successful.

Nevertheless, when success is our sole aim, it can cause us to do some very stupid things. In fact, when we focus only on the success, we can make it harder to achieve.

When I was in college, I met a younger guy going through the same program I was. Early in his college career, he had a great idea for a website. This was the beginning of the original dot-com boom. So, in the late 90s, he built a website that allowed high school students to connect with their alumni. A group of investors bought the website from this college student for approximately 1 million dollars, and he was just a sophomore!

That was a success, right? Well, maybe . . .

He left school and told us he lived on a boat for a year with his girlfriend. It is amazing how fast you can blow a million dollars. The next year he was back at school – broke – and saying if only he could come up with another website.

He needed to be successful again.

The second time he was not able to produce the same level of success. Instead of tapping into his creative juices to come up with the next big thing, he went to someone else's website and copied all the code. He then passed off the new website as his own and tried to sell it to another group of investors. Eventually, the authorities got involved and his opportunity to gain success ended.

Albert Einstein, one of the most famous physicists to ever live, said, "Try not to become a man of success, but rather try to become a man of value." Einstein was not asserting to run from success or even reject success.

What he so brilliantly communicated was that *our efforts, our striving, our trying, our ambition should not be toward the "success" of our work, but toward the "value" of it.*

You can almost hear Dorothy Sayers echoing Einstein, proclaiming we should serve the work and not the community. That instead of chasing success, we should chase the idea of value.

No matter what level of success you have achieved, freedom and meaning are found in the following idea: *No matter what you have achieved you can always learn, grow, and move.*

> *We do not measure ourselves on past success, but on the level of mastery we achieve each day as we move. Success is not the end. Mastery is the journey.*

We find more satisfaction in the *work* to produce the result or Living Visual than the actual end-product or state-of-being.

When we are creating, we find joy in the movement we experience in the *process*, versus the object we create. You can hear the echo of Coach Dabo's speech here, that life is made up of moments, and it's what we do in between that counts.

You can enjoy your marriage, even if it's not perfect, if you are making it better. You can enjoy your job, even if there are aspects of it that are less than ideal, if you are learning, growing, and contributing.

How depressing would life be if to achieve happiness we were required to reproduce one amazing moment after another? It's impossible.

Isn't it more refreshing to believe that you can find joy every day in the "grind" if you move toward mastery. When we move toward mastery it provides us peace, because we are moving, regardless of the recognition or success that the movement produces.

How do we create work that is valuable? How do we escape the success trap?

We set our minds on becoming masters. We deliberately practice our trade, art, skill, and talents until we reach a place where our work is valuable.

How refreshing! How liberating!

We don't have to chase success or try to repeat it. We are free from thinking that if we don't make it into a magazine or on the radio or television or to the White House that we are a failure. We now are free to move toward creating things of value.

Even when we have experienced success, isn't it refreshing to know that we aren't measured by our last commercial success, but for the value we create for others and how we improve ourselves?

Sarah Lewis discusses the idea of success versus mastery in her book, *The Rise,* where she tells of observing a college team of female archers. They would arrive at practice early and spend hours honing their craft. Lewis then compares archery to the difference between success and mastery by explaining that success is like hitting the target one time, while mastery is being able to hit the target consistently.[37]

When you pursue becoming a person of value, you focus on performing work with mastery. Focusing on mastery gives you the ability to pursue "excellence in obscurity". You are free to work without worrying about what the community thinks or whether you have achieved notoriety or fame. You become free to focus on increasing the value of your work. You enjoy more internal satisfaction mastering valuable work, even in obscurity, than stumbling into success without mastery.

When we create movement in our life, we should move toward creating, ordering, restoring, renewing, and growing things of value by pursuing mastery first.

How should we approach living a life of mastery?

First, we set high expectations of ourselves to operate in higher-order activities, serve the work, and pursue mastery.

Second, we expect little from the world around us.

Third, we deep-six any sense of entitlement. No one owes us anything. We earn everything.

Mindset #6 – Embrace Suffering

Theologians and philosophers have written and argued on the topic of suffering and evil for thousands of years. It is not my intent to fully develop the idea of suffering in the world and how it relates not only to humanity but to us, as individuals. My approach is more pragmatic.

The reality of our world is that suffering exists. We have a few choices in how we relate to or deal with suffering:

1. Run from it.
2. Ignore it.
3. Bemoan it.
4. Embrace it.

If we *run from suffering,* we chase pleasure. We blind ourselves from the suffering in the world and work extremely hard to eliminate any semblance of suffering from our lives.

Yet, no matter how successful we are at running from suffering, we will find that pleasure teaches us little. If we run from suffering, we are running from our own growth and development. Ironically, this lack of growth leads to more suffering.

If we *ignore suffering*, we trick ourselves into believing that all suffering is not real, that suffering only exists in our minds. Therefore, if we go deep enough, we may be able to find a place of inner peace without suffering.

However, the atrocities that occupy the front pages of the world every day should be impossible to ignore, and to do so might seem the ultimate savagery. Who could ignore suffering that was right before their eyes, sitting on their front step, or filling the streets of their city?

Any inner peace found in ignorance would be a false sense of security, leaving us unprepared, open to crippling responses and false realities.

If we *bemoan suffering*, we accept that it is real, but resign ourselves to believe that there is nothing we can do about it. It is what it is. Oh, how terrible, woe is me. Woe is us! The world is dark and cruel. Suffering is everywhere and solutions are nowhere to be found.

Even when suffering is comforted or eliminated, we bemoan the time it took or the way it was done or how it could be better. The glass is half-empty and suffering is always present. We are cemented to it and cannot move. It's terrifying. It's petrifying. It's too gloomy to bother. So, we sit.

Finally, it is possible to *embrace suffering*. We fully accept that suffering is part of the world in which we live and we all experience suffering in our lives. Yet instead of running, ignoring, or bemoaning, we embrace it. We move toward our suffering and grasp it. We wrestle with it. We struggle and try to understand it. We get closer to it each time we grapple.

Our goal is not to live in suffering. On the contrary, by embracing it, we can move through it. When we embrace suffering and move through it, we come out the other side different than before. We are changed in the process. We may be bruised, but we are stronger. Suffering heightens our awareness that we are alive. When we embrace suffering we embrace reality.

David Brooks writes masterfully about suffering in his book, *The Road to Character*. Brooks writes:

> *"For most of us, there is nothing intrinsically noble about suffering. Just as failure is sometimes just failure (and not your path to becoming the next Steve Jobs), suffering is sometimes just destructive, to be exited or medicated as quickly as possible. When it is not connected to some larger purpose beyond itself, suffering shrinks or annihilates people. When it is not understood as a piece of a larger process, it leads to doubt, nihilism, and despair.*
>
> *But some people can connect their suffering to some greater design. They place their suffering in solidarity with all the others who have suffered. These people are clearly ennobled by it. It is not the suffering itself that makes the difference, but the way it is experienced. Think of the way Franklin Roosevelt came back deeper and more empathetic after being struck by polio. Often, physical or social suffering can give people an outsider's perspective, an attuned awareness of what others are enduring."*[38]

Suffering changes us, if we embrace it.

Brooks continues:

> *"Suffering opens up ancient places of pain that had been hidden. It exposes frightening experiences that had been repressed, shameful wrongs that had been committed. It spurs some people to painfully and carefully examine the basement of their own soul. But it also presents the pleasurable sensation that one is getting closer to the truth. The pleasure in suffering is that you feel you are getting beneath the superficial and approaching the fundamental. It creates what modern psychologists call "depressive realism," an ability to see things exactly the way they*

are. It shatters the comforting rationalizations and pat narratives we tell about ourselves as part of our way of simplifying ourselves for the world."

What movie comes to mind when you read about the pleasure people feel in suffering, when they believe they are getting closer to the truth?

One movie that stands out to me is the Matrix. Neo, played by Keanu Reeves, lives inside the Matrix in relative comfort. Given a choice, he accepts the path of suffering because he wants to know the truth.

Suffering changes our perspective about the world and can open the door to understanding the truth about ourselves.

However, there is another major benefit realized when we suffer: Gratitude.

Brooks writes:

"Suffering, oddly, also teaches gratitude. In normal times we treat the love we receive as a reason for self-satisfaction (I deserve to be loved), but in seasons of suffering we realize how underserved this love is and how it should in fact be a cause for thanks. In proud moments we refuse to feel indebted, but in humble moments, people know they don't deserve the affection and concern they receive."

So, embrace suffering. Ironically, by doing so we create movement in ourselves and our lives. We see ourselves and the world with greater clarity. And clarity is the basis for movement.

Think back on experiences of suffering in your life. What did you gain from those experiences?

If the answer is nothing, evaluate your responses.

Suffering itself does not produce the benefits that Brooks described. It is our *response* to suffering that produces movement. You may be reading this book because you want to move away from a place of suffering. Embrace it. Move through it. Allow suffering to do the hard work of changing your perspective, increasing your nobility, truth, and gratitude.

Then, when you make it to the other side, the suffering will not have been in vain. On the contrary, you may even be grateful for the opportunity created through your suffering.

Mindset #7 – Mental Toughness

On October 15th, 2015, I wrote the following entry in my journal:

> I heard a great intro on a TED talk by Dan Ariclie, who teaches psychology at Duke. He said when you read books on mountain climbing do you find that they are full of joy and happiness? No, they are full of misery and hardship. They are full of frostbite and difficulty walking, difficulty breathing, with cold, challenging circumstances. If people were just trying to be happy when they got to the top, they would say this was a terrible idea! Let's go and find a warm beach to lay on have a refreshing drink. Instead, they (the mountain climbers) go down and recover, only to get back up and climb again.
>
> This suggests we care about the fight and rising to the challenge that motivates us.
>
> It (work) is more than just a paycheck. It is a cause, a purpose, a dragon, a mountain, an ocean. It is something to find or conquer . . .

What struck me about the TED talk is how often I overlook the need for challenges, and how often I pursue the beach over the mountain peak. I wrote that concept in my journal, so I would not forget the joy we have in facing the daily challenges, trials, and troubles. Without problems, there are no solutions. Without danger, there is no courage. Without suffering, there is no relief.

The example the Duke professor made during the TED talk also speaks to maintaining mental toughness during hard times.

When you create movement in your life, many times you face inertia from the world around you. When you push, the world pushes back.

It takes *resolve and discipline* to make it to the top of the mountain, regardless of what type of mountain you are climbing. Many times, when we move, it may require sacrifice or suffering to make it to where we want to be.

How do we maintain resolve in the midst of movement?

> **To maintain the Movement Mindset, you need to be inspired.**

So, how do you maintain the inspiration, energy and mental toughness in the face of difficulty?

Our Living Visual inspires us to move through the work at hand. Inspiration is all around us in other people's good deeds, the love of a child, the sunrise after a long or sleepless night. Allow yourself to be inspired.

When we connect our movement to a greater good, we find inspiration. If we believe the mastery of our work is part of a larger story and that our work produces something that moves the world just a little in the right direction, we can tough out the difficult days.

Framing failure is another skill that is necessary for maintaining mental toughness.

We determined earlier that success is not a destination, but marks along a journey. Failure shouldn't be a destination either, but just some battle scars or wounds that teach us along the way. We only fail when we stop moving or give up. As long as we are still moving, our failures, scars and wounds become badges of honor. And when you look at all the difficulties you have been through, to make it where you are today, it is inspiring.

If we can find inspiration in our movement, in the world around us, and even in our own failings, then we can move with confidence and mental toughness.

~~~~

Earlier in the book, I wrote about my experience playing music and having to decide whether to move to Nashville. On one of our trips there, we met Herky Williams in his office at ASCAP (a not-for-profit performance-rights organization). Herky knew a lot of songwriters in the industry, and the meeting had been set up by an A&R rep at Universal Records.

My wife and I sat down across from Herky and – no joke – the first words out of his mouth were: "Have you tried out for the Tennessee Titans yet?"

I would love to say that he asked me that question because I look like a natural-born, pro-athlete. Unfortunately, my 6-foot, 190-pound frame mostly screams slow-white-dude.

I sat up and firmly said, "No, sir . . ."

He then proceeded to explain why it was statistically more likely for me to make it playing professional football than becoming a songwriter. It was brutal. I had never met Herky, and he had never heard my songs.

After telling me all the mathematical impossibilities in becoming a professional songwriter, he listened to just a few seconds of one of my songs, and proclaimed, "You don't have the 'essence.' " Never mind the fact that an A&R rep from Universal Records (the person who offers record deals) had set up the meeting, because she thought my songs were great! What a rollercoaster!

My point in this little story is that there are 100,000 people in Nashville, or any other town, that will tell you "no" (Herky may have said the same to Lee Brice or Garth Brooks) and rejection stinks, but how we **respond** to rejection is what makes the difference.

I left Herky's office without feeling disappointed. Maybe it was because I had been in sales and had faced being turned down. That experience had taught me not to take rejection personally, but instead maintain mental toughness and keep moving.

~~~~

My father grew up, the youngest of four children, on a tenant farm. His father did not own the home they lived in. The family was extremely poor. Some of his stories about growing up with no indoor plumbing, using an out-house, seeing his breath fog into the air while laying in bed on cold nights, and working in the fields all day are amazing. They sound like something you would hear about a family living in the 1800s, than life in the 1950s.

My dad always said that, growing up, his goal was to provide his family with a home that had air conditioning and indoor plumbing. He worked five jobs (at the same time) when I was young.

One of those jobs was a business he had started with his brothers. In the early years, they developed a new technology and were eager to pitch it to engineers. Time after time he would visit engineers and they would either insult him or laugh his technology out of their office. He knew it was superior to anything on the market and within a few years, it started to take off. Now, it is one of the most highly regarded systems of its kind in the country by some of the largest engineering firms.

How could my father take so many "no's"?

I believe part of it goes back to his childhood and the idea of **What do you have to lose?** He had seen the bottom and it was all up from there. His family lived in a home with a/c and indoor plumbing – the rest was gravy (as they say in the south).

My father overcame some significant obstacles in his life and career with hard work and mental toughness. Without realizing it, he had used six simple steps to maintain a Movement Mindset.

And I'm glad he did.

Chapter 13

Turning the Flywheel

It's hard to beat a person who never gives up.

— Babe Ruth

Take the first step

The last chapter on Execution is written to encourage and motivate. Executing with intention is hard work and takes a lot of energy.

Sometimes we may avoid the work because of how difficult we perceive it will be. I don't know how long I had ideas for writing a book, but it was at least 10 years – and I never wrote a single line. It wasn't until I intentionally set aside some consistent time, committed to the process, and typed out an outline that the book began.

> ✴ **Change your response, change your life.**

How easy is that?

It may sound cliché, but it's true. For 10 years I was full of excuses: I am not a good writer; I don't have any free time; I need more ideas; and so on and so on. I was an excuse factory.

Remember the example in the first part of the book about the smoker? Once they saw smoking cigarettes for what it was, they didn't want it anymore. They just stopped being a smoker.

Well, once I created a mental image of this book, sitting on a bookshelf and leading someone to become more of who they were made to be, all the excuses seemed trivial. I became a writer. I believed that I could help people by writing a book. I found the time, committed to writing, and forgot the rest of my excuses.

Sometimes it is easy to blame our parents, brother, sisters, teachers, boss, coworkers, or other people for creating our attitudes. However, if we believe that we control our responses, then we reject the notion that our problems are someone else's fault and take responsibility for choosing our attitude and responses.

And most of all, we begin to believe that we have the power to move – to take the first step.

Marcus Aurelius, the great stoic and Emperor of Rome said, *"You have power over your mind – not outside events. Realize this, and you will find strength."*

We have the power to change, but we must choose to take personal responsibility. This book has covered all the necessary tools to help us execute with intention. Now it is time to take the first step. It takes courage to take the first step, even if it's a small one. However, it is easier than you think.

Consistent Micro-Moves

Movement is taking the first step in the direction of the intentional future you. By taking the first step, it makes it easier to take the second. Also, as we move, we also affect others. Our lives have ripples that go through our friends, family, co-workers, and community.

Jim Collins' best-selling book, *Good to Great*, masterfully likens inertia in business to a flywheel. This is how that concept is described:

Picture a huge, heavy flywheel – a massive metal disk mounted horizontally on an axle, about 30 feet in diameter, 2 feet thick, and weighing about 5,000 pounds. Now imagine that your task is to get the flywheel rotating on the axle as fast and long as possible.

Pushing with great effort, you get the flywheel to inch forward, moving almost imperceptibly at first. You keep pushing and, after two or three hours of persistent effort, you move it around a second rotation.

You keep pushing in a consistent direction.

Three turns . . . four . . . five . . . six . . . the flywheel builds up speed . . . seven . . . eight . . . you keep pushing . . . nine . . . ten . . . it builds momentum . . . eleven . . . twelve . . . moving faster with each turn . . . twenty . . . thirty . . . fifty . . . a hundred.

Then at some point – breakthrough!

The momentum of the thing kicks in your favor, hurling the flywheel forward, turn after turn . . . whoosh! Its own heavyweight is working for you. You are pushing no harder than the first rotation, but the flywheel goes faster and faster.[39]

Doing little things adds up to big things. It is the power of small steps. The first step makes the second easier.

When I was in high school, the football team would begin practice two weeks before school started. We called the practices "2-a-days" because we had a morning and an afternoon practice every day. Even though we lifted weights and spent hours in throwing drills and agility exercises, my first week of varsity practice was brutal.

I will never forget the feeling I had when I woke up the morning after our first practice. I opened my eyes and the sun was rising. I was excited about the new day, ready to get to practice.

Then, I tried to move, but my body refused. I was almost worried, but soon realized that just about every muscle in my body was sore. If it wasn't sore from running, it was sore from hitting all the amazing athletes who were bigger, faster and stronger than me.

It took me about 5 minutes to get out of bed. I never sat up. I had to roll over and land on my feet.

I contemplated what would happen if I just got back in the bed and the voices started chiming in: "Dallas, you are never going to play pro ball, so what does it matter?" "Dallas, you are never going to play Division 1 college ball, so why put yourself through the pain?" "Dallas, you may not even start this year, is it worth it?" "Give up, call in sick, take a break, stop!"

I admit that first morning I was tempted to get back in bed!

Taking the first step to go brush my teeth was torture. Then I took another and another. By the time I got to practice, I had worked a lot of the soreness out, and after talking with my teammates, I learned that they had felt the same way.

Sadly, a few guys didn't show back up. The voices in their heads got to them.

I never played pro or college ball. My junior year I never saw the field on Friday nights. So, the voices in my head were not completely inaccurate! "You are never going to play . . ." could have been the difference.

But when you **don't give yourself the liberty to choose to quit**, and you are turning that flywheel really slow, the response is: I may never play in college or the pros, **but I can play today**. I am building momentum today for tomorrow.

I had so much fun being a part of a winning team. Learning the game of football. Building relationships with friends, and ultimately, starting on Friday nights my senior year.

It all began with rolling out of bed and trudging to brush my teeth on day 2 of our 2-a-days.

For me, football was a small step in character development. It taught me perseverance, teamwork, self-discipline, and how to get up after being knocked down. It was one of my micro-moves toward getting to where and who I wanted to be.

What micro moves are building your character? How are you challenging yourself every day? Where is your flywheel? Is it in the early struggle to create just an inch of movement or is it moving with tremendous speed?

My friend Randy is a retired fighter pilot. He even looks like a fighter pilot. I have never met Randy out at a restaurant, movies, cookout or another event when his hair was not perfectly and tightly cut. His clothes are always neatly pressed. He has sharp eyes that just seem to be made to focus. I enjoy talking with him about his career in the Air Force and philosophy on life.

One thing that Randy said is that he believes your bed should be made first thing every morning. He was extremely adamant about it. I asked if his life and time in the military had established that regimented habit and pictured the many scenes in army movies where everyone is lined up in the barracks for bed inspection by a screaming sergeant. However, Randy said that was not the case at all. He takes it so seriously because making the bed is a little accomplishment that starts the day with positive progress.

Randy starts every day feeling like he has already accomplished something.

Is making your bed a big item to check off on the long to-do list of the day? No . . . That's why so many people don't take the time to do it. But for Randy, it's the first turn on his daily flywheel.

Maybe your day starts without making your bed. But why not take control and start it with a win to establish some momentum for the day?

When we want to create movement in our life, we have to accept the reality of our lives and decide we need to take a step.

My wife likes running in the morning. I enjoy spending time in meditation and prayer. Do the little things and push the flywheel.

Want to change the world? It may start by making your bed!

The goal is not to produce massive results. Be patient. Just move the ball one yard, then another, then another. As you build momentum, your consistent micro-moves will become smoother

221

and faster. Your flywheel will start to gain energy, and then your movement will be greater and easier to sustain.

Why are micro-moves so powerful?

1. They encourage consistency. Consistency leads to change.
2. They build momentum, like the flywheel example in the book, *Good to Great*.
3. They develop positive habits.
4. They generate micro-wins. Winning builds confidence.
5. They give us time to review our progress and direction.
6. They give us needed feedback.

Win the Day

Can we agree that some days life seems like a drudge? I am not talking about our "my life is amazing" Facebook or Instagram persona. I am talking about life when we wake up with a stomach virus, realize our work isn't very fulfilling, or make a blunder when we should have known better.

Sometimes we lose the wonder of a child and the world looks gray. To make matters worse, we see other people's lives online and think, "What am I doing wrong?" We begin to believe that everyone else has found the keys to happiness and success, while we are stuck in a rut.

Relax. No one is happy all the time or has a perfect life, no matter what they put on Instagram.

The real question is **how you deal with the daily grind.**

Earlier in the book, we covered the amazing story of the Clemson victory in the National Championship. Millions of people watched that moment. Sports Illustrated published not one, but two covers of the game. It was definitely a Facebook or Instagram moment. "Look, mom; I am holding the trophy! We did it!"

However, it is not surprising that fewer people tuned into the White House Channel when the team was invited to come and visit the President of the United States. During their visit, Dabo Swinney was given the opportunity to make a speech. Dabo, like so many other leaders and movers, had an interesting view on the "special moment" of winning the National Championship:

". . . And I just, I wanna make a message really to our players. Because this is, this is a special moment. Ya know, back in January, that was an incredible moment. What a moment, January 9th, into the 10th actually, what an incredible moment that was.

And then I had a chance to see a lot of these guys put those caps and gowns on and become graduates of Clemson University. What a special moment.

Some of 'em have already taken jobs, getting their first paycheck. Special moment.

Some of these guys have signed with NFL teams. What a special moment.

Being here at the White House as the nation's champion? What a special moment.

But I want you players to know that there's going to be other special moments. There's going to be other special moments— when you get married, when you become a father, when you buy that first house. There's going to be other special moments.

Ten years from now, we're going to have a special moment when we have a reunion. Some of you are going to be bald, some of you are going to have big bellies. But it's goin' be a special moment when we get back together.

But I want you all to know, all you players, and really everyone, **life is not about those moments. Life is truly about how we live between the moments.** *That's really what it comes down to. It's all about how we live between the moments. It's just doing the little things in a great way. It's the daily focus and purpose and commitment and attitude that you choose to embrace every single day between those moments.*

That's what we're all going to be defined by."[40]

Coach Dabo knows one of the keys to movement. You must win the day. You must choose to be great when life is a grind. When the players are in the hot southern sun, sweating it out in August and no crowds are watching, they still put in maximum effort.

Time in the grind will determine who you are much more than the moment in the spotlight.

When we realize that it is the daily battles that make the difference, we begin to realize how important our mindset is each day and how important winning the day becomes.

Maybe we could change the way we look at the "grind." The word itself may change. When we read the word "grind," do we think of gears grinding us to a pulp each day? Or coarse sandpaper grinding us down to dust? Remember Mindset #6: Embrace Suffering gives us the mental perspective we need to respond to "the grind." When we realize that the grind is what gives us a chance to produce the most amazing future version of our self, the word takes on new meaning.

Like a craftsman grinding away the excess raw stone to expose the beautiful diamond beneath or the sculptor grinding away unnecessary rock to reveal a stunning statue, drudgery has a purpose. Daily problems turn into opportunities.

As we work through the drudgery found between the amazing moments of our lives we develop routines and habits.

What habits or routines consistently keep us from reaching our potential? Maybe watching too much TV, hurting others with our words when we are stressed, spending too much time on social media, or forgetting to make up our beds?

> ✶ **We are what we consistently do.**

If we want to *Win the Day*, we must build healthy habits and routines and break poor habits. Here are two tips for breaking poor habits:

1. Stop rewarding the poor habit or find the same reward in a good habit.
2. Start a new positive habit to take the place of a poor habit.

When we take control of our routines and habits, we can consistently *Win the Day* and live well in the drudgery between the moments. Be great — today.

Do not worry about the legacy of your life or your career. Instead focus on moving, just one day. Today!

Take Stock

When we take stock, it is not to check a box. Think about a grocery store. When the grocery employee counts how many cans of beans they have on the shelf, it drives a response. If they have too few cans, the store responds by ordering more. If they have too many, the store responds by not ordering more or changing to a brand that customers like better.

When you move, take stock.

A very successful CEO, mentor, and good friend of mine used to always tell me: "You can't manage what you don't measure." And this advice has served me well in business. However, taking stock is useless if it doesn't drive change. The natural follow-up phrase to my friend's quote is ". . . and you need to manage what you do measure!"

Think about the following questions. When we execute, we constantly take stock of the results we are producing.

Do my actions align with my initial Living Visual?
Has that picture changed?
Am I executing within my boundaries?

Am I receiving valuable feedback from my accountability systems?

If your spouse or best friend mentioned that you have an anger management problem, what would you do? Would you brush it off? Would you ask for specific examples? Ironically, would you get angry?

What would be great is if you could identify the times you became angry, what triggered it, and then work on ways that your spouse or friend could hold you accountable to keep cool.

If we brush it off, we can't move.

If we get angry, we haven't moved.

If we listen to someone who cares about us and take stock of our life, we have a greater chance of moving and overcoming our anger.

> ✴ **When we take stock, we tie what we know to be true to movement.**

When we find something that aligns with our skills and talents, we gain energy from the action. When we accomplish something, it gives us a sense of pride, a natural high.

Why is this not movement?

The whole of Pillar IV is about execution, and now we have decided that accomplishing things is not movement?

Well, without taking stock, we don't know if our work is producing the product we set out to create. <u>Execution is not movement, in and of itself.</u> It takes clarity, boundaries, and accountability to ensure our execution has purpose. Using the concepts in MOVE! we understand that *Intentional* Execution is more powerful than execution alone.

In his book *The 7 Habits of Highly Effective People*, Stephen Covey describes execution alone as the difference between leadership and management. He tells the story of a crew of workers that have been tasked with clearing brush and trees in a forest or jungle.[41] They work hard putting systems into place and become excellent at clearing debris.

Finally, one of the men climbs to the top of the trees and shouts to the crew: "Wrong jungle!" The team shouts back: "Shut-up! We're making great progress!"

Execution without comprehensive thought.

When we take stock, we are gathering information and comparing that information against our clarity, boundaries and accountability structures. The information produces a feedback loop that allows us to make adjustments based on the reality of what we are facing, how we are progressing, or the results we are achieving. The feedback helps us execute with **intention**.

Think about some of the crises in your life.

Were you cutting trees in the right jungle? Did those crises come from activities that were truly important and in alignment with your core purpose and desires?

Ask the same question the manufacturing worker was asked when building the new APEX line: "How do I know I have been successful today?"

Take stock.

~~~~

If the engine of the plane were to burn all its fuel at once, it might go fast for a time short time, but not make it to the next airport. If it doesn't use enough fuel at takeoff, it never makes it off the ground.

Our emotions and attitudes are great strengths when we use them to our advantage. If we are struggling to overcome obstacles and barriers, but we know it is for a great cause, our attitudes and emotions give us the energy to finish strong. However, if we burn all our energy out at the beginning of any opportunity, we may not have enough to reach the finish line.

Herein lies a paradox of accountability.

In the previous section, we discussed the need to detach from your movement so that you can see clearly, without emotions clouding your judgment. However, once you have taken stock, and know what needs to be accomplished, it boosts your emotional connection to the tasks you need to accomplish and the movements you are making.

> **Taking stock gives your movement purpose. It ensures energy is intentionally directed.**

As you see more results, you become more passionate about movement. Taking stock loops the results of your action back through clarity, boundaries, and accountability. When you are moving and take stock, it reinforces every step you take to achieve your Living Visual.

Why?

Because when you take stock, you see progress, and progress makes you feel good. You are moving a little closer to your potential. You have proof when you take stock.

Think about the reality show, *The Biggest Loser*. Contestants begin the show overweight and often with bad attitudes. Then, they hit the wall at some point and want to quit the show. But, as they progress and start to take stock of how much weight they have lost and how much better they feel, it propels them to move even further.

The same is true for all of us. Don't run from accountability, elevate it in your life. Take stock.

Years ago, I was researching our family heritage. My ancestors are from Scotland, and the family crest reads "Courage Flourishes at the Wound" and speaks to movement.

When we move, sometimes it will be messy, painful and difficult. Sometimes we row in the rain and wind and sometimes we row in sunny weather. However, the Five Paths, and maintaining the Movement Mindset, help frame our progress while we exert energy and turn our life's flywheel.

If we get muddy or hurt while executing something difficult, we can acknowledge it and learn from it but keep moving!

Control fear with clarity and let courage lead you. Force your emotions to work for you. Take stock and **believe that your seat on the row boat is headed right where you want to go**.

Questions

- What is one thing (no matter how small) you can do right now to move closer to where you want to be?
- Do you believe that consistent investment in something for 15 minutes every day will help you?
- What can you give 15 minutes to every day that will help you Intentionally Execute?

Pillar IV Review

We have come to the end of Pillar IV of the book, which focused on the Five Paths traveled to create movement, the Movement Mindsets necessary to execute, and finally, learning the art of turning our flywheel of life.

Chapter 11 communicated the idea of the types of execution we can be intentional in performing. We learned about the Five Paths which are used:

1. To Create
2. To Restore
3. To Renew
4. To Order
5. To Grow

These five paths helped us better understand the varieties of results we can produce by overlapping one or more of the Five Paths.

Chapter 12 presented the seven Movement Mindsets, which taught us how to utilize specific mental tools as we move.

Mindset #1 – Prepare for Opportunity
Mindset #2 – Slow is Smooth, Smooth is Fast
Mindset #3 – Serve the Work (not the community)
Mindset #4 – Value Flexibility
Mindset #5 – Success vs. Mastery
Mindset #6 – Embrace Suffering
Mindset #7 – Mental Toughness

The Movement Mindsets helped us frame how we think, in order to sustain long-term, successful movement.

Chapter 13 covered some motivational ideas and best practices to help improve our movement. We learned the importance of small victories and the necessity of taking stock of the results of our movement. We also learned the paradox of accountability and how to use it to detach and re-attach our emotions to our movement.

Chapter 14

The End, The Beginning

And in the end, it's not the years in your life that count. It's the life in your years.

— Abraham Lincoln

———————————

A few years ago, Liberty Mutual came out with a "Pay It Forward" commercial that opens with a young lady standing on a street corner who saves a pizza delivery boy from walking out into traffic. A man sitting in a café booth across the street notices her selfless act, and in the next scene, he is shown helping a woman and her baby get off the bus. His act of kindness is noticed by someone else, who performs yet another act of goodwill.

The commercial follows the domino movement created by inspired acts of kindness until it ends with the original woman viewing an act of kindness, who then stops the pizza delivery guy from walking out into traffic.

It is a feel-good commercial that perfectly captured the "pay it forward" theme. The challenge forces us to think about how we can display that trait, or how we were made to change the world for the better.

Just thinking about this opens us up to opportunities to become part of this theme.

In the commercial, the woman stopped the pizza boy, which was noticed by the man in the café, who was then inspired or challenged.

However, he did not run to the same corner and wait for the next unaware pizza boy to save from traffic. No, instead, he left the café and sometime later was presented with a situation that allowed him to respond using his unique gifts and talents.

Be inspired. Notice the grandeur of life. Notice the amazing little things that people do. Recapture the wonder you had as a child and let that inspirational power drive you to MOVE!

It is hard work, but if you create movement with your unique gifts and talents, the ripple will have a greater effect than you could ever imagine.

You have what you need to create movement in your life. You had it when you picked up this book. Now, you have tools and understanding and the roadmap to unlock your potential and MOVE!

At the beginning of our journey, we developed the idea of white spaces we face in our lives. What do we do when up is down and down is up? We learned four concepts that give stability and direction to our white spaces and are fundamental to the idea of movement:

- Seek Clarity
- Develop Boundaries
- Elevate Accountability
- Intentionally Execute

Remember, most people resist change – and movement is change. Don't be surprised when you decide to create movement and find obstacles placed in your path. Don't be discouraged with slow progress. Sometimes the world seems to be working against us or holding us back from achieving our goals, but there is always something you can move: *Yourself*.

If you believe that movement is always possible, then you believe that moving toward your potential is always possible. Moving toward your potential goes a long way in creating a life full of satisfaction and happiness.

The Difference

I was living in Atlanta and working with a corporate training company. I had been in a meeting at Home Depot's headquarters and was headed back to the office. I was listening to the radio and the announcer came on and made a comment about Tiger Woods earnings. He said Tiger Woods was the highest-earning golfer in the world, which made me curious about the value of being the absolute best versus being almost the best.

In 2007, Tiger Woods earnings were approximately $112 million.[42] How much better was Tiger than the rest of the field?

I remembered seeing him dominate out so many tournaments and figured his average score would be 5 strokes lower than the rest of the field.

Phil Mickelson was Tiger's greatest rival at the time and his stroke average was 69.46.[43]

In comparison, Tiger Woods' stroke average was 67.79.[44]

A difference of only 1.67 strokes per tournament for the year.

What is 1.67 strokes worth in professional golf? Compared to Tiger's $112 million, Phil earned $51 million the same year. Being the absolute best was worth about $61 million, or more than double the worth of being almost the best.

How close is close enough?

My intent in using this analogy is not to praise Tiger or in some way infer that Phil was not giving his absolute maximum effort. Both players are elite, world-class golfers and always put their all into the game of golf.

The big idea here is that every day we decide whether to give our absolute best or something less.

Putting forth *"almost"* our best effort can **dramatically affect the return on our efforts**.

Our story is not about two competing pro-golfers, but two competing futures. Our best produces one future, while anything less produces another. We decide to move with intention and excellence – or stay stagnant.

When just a sliver of effort separates almost the best from being the best, don't allow excuses –

> I'll start tomorrow . . .
> It doesn't matter . . .
> I can always get by . . .
> It's no big deal if I don't . . .
> That looks too hard . . .
> That's too risky . . .
> I'd never be successful . . .
>
> — to make your choices.

Don't settle for an almost-great career or an almost-great marriage or an almost-healthy lifestyle or an almost-close relationship with your kids.

The difference between where you are and where you want to be might just be *_this_* close.

So, honor the fact that you were made to move. Grab the power that is already in you, just waiting for you to develop it.

One thing is for certain, **when you choose to MOVE! – it will change your life.**

From the author:

It's been over two years since I began writing this book on movement. My hope is that the stories, advice, and questions contained within these pages will help you reorient your life towards creating meaningful movement and confidently face the challenging "Now what?" moments in your life's journey. Applying the concepts in this book have proved invaluable to my family and me.

For more information on how to become a *Thriver*, join our community, discover additional content, sign up for retreats, learn about our consulting solutions, or to book Dallas Burnett for a speaking engagement visit www.ThinkMoveThrive.com.

ThinkMove**Thrive**

Experiencing suffering and tribulation reveals how all humans are alike. How we choose to respond and learn from those experiences is what makes us all unique.

– Dallas Burnett

Acknowledgments

Your best work is not "your" work, but your skills and talents rolled up in the combined efforts of a great team. MOVE! would not be possible without the efforts of many people. I would like to thank everyone who has offered encouragement because this world has so little of it. First, I would like to thank my Mom and Dad. They gave me a great moral example, supportive family, and work ethic. Taking risks were encouraged at home and have served me well throughout my career. Mom, I am sure you never thought that those late-night proofreading sessions and grammar lessons would one day produce a book!

I would like to thank people specifically related to the writing, design, production, and distribution of MOVE! To Maria D'Marco, my editor, thank you! Your insights were tremendous and helped simplify my message increase its clarity. Matt New, not only designed the cover but the interior graphics as well. He is an incredible graphic artist and my good friend. Matt and I have partnered in all kinds of projects over the years. He gets me! Many thanks to his creativity and hard work in helping bring the book to life. To my awesome proofreadering team: Michael, Jeff, Louis, Leslie, and Randy, I appreciate your time, expertise and advice on the fine-tuning of MOVE! I would not have been able to finish the book without your help and feedback. Finally, thank you Andrew Tennant for laying out and typesetting the book and for working hard to finish on my tight publishing schedule.

Here are some other people who indirectly influenced me and the writing of this book. Thank you to one of my mentors Louis Alderman, who has always been a constant encourager. His storytelling ability was incredible, but his desire to help me overcome challenges in work and life was even more amazing. He always demonstrated a servant's heart to me and gave me wise professional counsel. He is a great coach. He has been and still is a great mentor. I would also like to thank Tim Grant who gave me opportunity and believed in me; and Charles Wall for taking time to tell me the truth, not just what I wanted to hear. Thanks to the original team that were part of piloting the material: DuBose, Kaley, Mariano, and Nickie, you all are the best!

Two people I coached around the same time responded so positively to the early material of this book encouraged me to take the plunge and turn the concepts into MOVE! Nickie, I hope that this book can continue to be an encouragement to you and Micah-Baby. Jim, I hope that you are able to use some of the material in this book in your new role. Thank you for giving me the opportunity to be a part of your lives.

Thanks to Jeff Rosenlund and Don Oglesby for giving me two great interviews. Thanks to Kevin who was the physician that discovered I had appendicitis. A big thanks to Lee Brice for taking time to hang out with me on one of his tours. I am proud of what you have accomplished, and the clarity you had back in college was amazing.

Finally, I would like to thank my wife for the hours of time she invested in late-night rereads, discussions, and edits of MOVE! Without her encouragement, I would have never finished the project. You have been a source of encouragement and a true partner through the entire project. Also, a big thanks to my daughters, Eva, Ellis, and Everli. Thank you for not minding when daddy had to sneak away to his office to write. Your energy is infectious, and I love you very much.

Endnotes

Introduction
1 Lewis, C. (1940). *The Problem of Pain*. New York, New York: Harper Collins.

Chapter 1
2 Brewer, J. A. (2013, Jun). Craving to Quit: Psychological Models and Neurobiological Mechanisms of Mindfulness Training as Treatment for Addictions. *Psychology of Addictive Behaviors*, 366-79.
3 CNN. (2005, December 30). *Transcripts CNN Larry King Live*. Retrieved from http://edition.cnn.com/: http://edition.cnn.com/TRANSCRIPTS/0512/30/lkl.01.html

Pillar I: Seek Clarity
4 Oxford University Press. (2016, 10 6). *Oxford Living Dictionary*. Retrieved from https://en.oxforddictionaries.com: https://en.oxforddictionaries.com/definition/clarity
5 Harvard Business Reveiw. (2014, 11 20). *Making Good Decisions*. Retrieved from https://hbr.org: https://hbr.org/2014/11/making-good-decisions

Chapter 2
6 Covey, S. R. (1989). *The 7 Habits of Highly Effective People*. New York, New York: Simon & Schuster.
7 Rasmussen, C. M. (2014). *The Momement of Clarity: Using the Human Sciences to Solve Your Toughest Business Problems*. Boston: Harvard Business Review Press.
8 LEGO Group. (2015). *The LEGO Group 2015 Annual Report*. Denmark: LEGO Group.

Chapter 3
9 Klein, G. (1998). *Sources of Power – How People Make Decisions*. Cambridge, Massachusetts: The MIT Press.
10 Burton, L. (1894). *Life of Sir Richard Burton*.
11 Berinato, S. (2016, June). Visualizations That Really Work. *Harvard Business Review*, 92–100.
12 Everitt, A. (2012). *The Rise of Rome – The Making of The Worlds Greatest Empire*. New York: Random House.
14 Epstein, D. (2013). *The Sports Gene : Inside The Science of Extrordinary Athletic Performance*. New York: Penguin Group.

Chapter 5

15 Covey, S. R. (1989). *The 7 Habits of Highly Effective People*. New York, New York: Simon & Schuster.

16 Lilley, S. (2012, November 1). From Rockets to Ruins "The PEPCON Ammonium Perchlorate Plant Explosion". *Monthly Safety e-Message, Volume 6*(Issue 9), pp. 1-4.

17 Lambert, H. a. (2003, July 2003). The PEPCON Disaster – Causative Factors and Potential Preventivive and Mitigative Measures. *Four International Seminar "Fire and Explosion Hazards*. Londondaery: Lawrence Livermore National Laboratory, U.S. Department of Energy.

Chapter 6

18 Dan Fuehrer, C. F. (2014, August 12). *Runners World – Runners With More Training Miles Finish Marathons Faster*. Retrieved from https://www.runnersworld.com/: https://www.runnersworld.com/training/a20807557/runners-with-more-training-miles-finish-marathons-faster/

19 Satell, G. (2014, September 05). A Look Back At Why Blockbuster Really Failed And Why It Didn't Have To Forbes. Retrieved from Forbes: https://www.forbes.com/sites/gregsatell/2014/09/05/a-look-back-at-why-blockbuster-really-failed-and-why-it-didnt-have-to/#5ddefefa1d64

20 Roy F. Baumeister, N. a.-G. (2014). Relevance of Willpower Dynamics, Self-Control, and Ego Depletion to Flawed Student Decision Making. *International Journal of Education and Social Science* , 147-150.

Chapter 7

21 Kennedy, J. F. (1961, 5 25). *NASA – Excerpt from the 'Special Message to the Congress on Urgent National Needs*. Retrieved from NASA: https://www.nasa.gov/vision/space/features/jfk_speech_text.html#.VWIGJ0_tmkp

Chapter 8

22 Oglesby, D. (2016, August 12). President/CEO. (D. Burnett, Interviewer)

23 Whiskey Disks. (2011, May 11). *Whiskey Apacalypse*. Retrieved from blog.whiskeydisks.com: http://blog.whiskeydisks.com/whiskey-apocalypse/

24 cbsnews.com Staff. (2000, May 9th). *Bourbon and Smoke*. Retrieved from www.cbsnews.com: http://www.cbsnews.com/news/bourbon-and-smoke/

25 Bertram, Charles. 6/25/2014. May 2000 Warehouse Fire at Wild Turkey. Retrieved from http://herald-leader.mycapture.com/mycapture/enlarge.asp?image=52174611&event=1817819&CategoryID=56922. (Image printed with permission from Lexington Herald Leader.)

Chapter 9

26 Rosenlund, J. (2016, June 2). Director of Client Engagement. (D. Burnett, Interviewer)

27 Fineran, L. (2013, January 3rd). *Two men charged after bungled jewellery store heist left them inside fast-food store*. Retrieved from The Courier Mail: http://www.couriermail.com.au/news/queensland/two-men-charged-after-bungled-jewellery-store-heist-left-them-inside-fast-food-store/news-story/a8de87f16818970e8823eedd80e458cf

ENDNOTES

Chapter 11
28 Achor, S. (2010). *The Happiness Advantage.* New York: Random House.
29 Brooks, D. (2015). *The Road to Character.* New York: Random House.
30 Harnish, V. (2012). *The Greatest Business Decisions of All Time.* New York, New York: Fortune Books.
31 Marchione, M. (2017, 12 3). *Scientific breakthrough: Phoenix-area man 1st to have genes edited.* Retrieved from https://www.azcentral.com: https://www.azcentral.com/story/news/local/arizona-health/2017/11/26/scientific-breakthrough-phoenix-area-man-1st-have-genes-edited/886231001/
32 Torre, P. S. (2009, March 23). How (and why) Athletes Go Broke. *Sports Illustrated.*

Chapter 12
33 ClemsonTigers.com. (2015, August 19). *Clemson Football | | New Scholarships.* Retrieved from YouTube: https://www.youtube.com/watch?v=NuPViLzyiME
34 Sayer, D. (1942). *Why Work?* London: Methuen.
35 Boddie, W. W. (1879). *Traditions of the Swamp Fox.* Spartanburg: The Reprint Company, Publishers.
36 Oller, J. (2016). *The Swamp Fox: how Francis Marion saved the American Revolution.* Boston: Da Capo Press.
37 Lewis, S. (2014). *The Rise.* New York: Simon & Schuster Paperbacks.
38 Brooks, D. (2015). *The Road to Character.* New York: Random House.

Chapter 13
39 Collins, J. C. (2001). *Good to Great: Why Some Companies Make the Leap . . . and Others Don't.* New York: HarperBusiness.
40 ACC Digital Network. (2017, June 12). *Dabo Swinney's Speech at Clemson's White House Visit.* Retrieved from YouTube: https://www.youtube.com/watch?v=YJthIqp52yw
41 Covey, S. R. (1989). *The 7 Habits of Highly Effective People.* New York, New York: Simon & Schuster.
42 Wood, R. (2017, July 30). *Sports Illustrated 2007 World 10.* Retrieved from Topend Sports: http://www.topendsports.com/world/lists/earnings/world-10-2007.htm
43 PGA. (2017, July 30). *PGA Players .* Retrieved from Phil Mickelson: http://www.pgatour.com/players/player.01810.phil-mickelson.html
44 PGA. (2017, July 30). *PGA Players.* Retrieved from Tiger Woods: http://www.pgatour.com/players/player.08793.tiger-woods.html

www.ingramcontent.com/pod-product-compliance
Lightning Source LLC
Chambersburg PA
CBHW021848090426
42811CB00033B/2187/J